The Witching Path

Moira Stirling

www.capallbann.co.uk

The Witching Path

©Copyright Moira Stirland 2006

ISBN 186163 275 4

ALL RIGHTS RESERVED

No part of this publication may be reproduced, stored in a retrieval system or transmitted in any form or by any means, electronic, mechanical, photocopying, scanning, recording or otherwise without the prior written permission of the author and the publisher.

Cover design by Paul Mason

Published by:

Capall Bann Publishing
Auton Farm
Milverton
Somerset
TA4 1NE

Dedication

My thanks and love are due to Karl Stirland, Chris Brinded, Nadine Angela, Liam, Hilda & John Dolan and to Phoebe and the rest of my family for their continuing love, support, kinship

To the Linden Wood Coven and all my wonderful friends, especially Jan, Jessica and Donna, for your encouragement and loving support, thank you, I love you all.

Contents

1 Introduction   3
A brief overview of Wicca and the most frequently asked questions answered for the novice.

2 Ethics   14
The Wiccan Rede and boomerang effect.

3 Creating Sacred Space   18
The Wiccan altar, the magic circle and invoking the elements. Cleansing and grounding.

4 The Tools of Wicca   33
How to cleanse and use sacred tools. Covering the wand, athame, besom, rattles, drums and others.

5 Energy Work and the Cone of Power   49
Techniques for raising energy in the circle, sensing auras and chakra work. The web of life.

6 The Sacred Journey   70
Undertaking Journey with clear instructions, the Place of Power and the Inner Guide.

7 The God and Goddess   82
A brief overview of Wiccan deity and journey to meet with their essence.

8 The Elements of Wicca   93
Earth, air, fire, water, spirit and their importance in Wicca.

9 Environmental Activism   134
Protest, campaigning and how it relates to Wicca and the elements.

10 Cycles and Seasons   **139**
Rituals for the eight Celtic festivals and the moon phases.

11 The Haberdashery for Spells and Ritual   **153**
Combining imagination and knowledge to pick out items for spells, from candles to pine cones.

12 Spells for Peace and Happiness   **158**
A selection of pre-formed spells for the reader to use or adapt.

1

Introduction

The fast-paced life of today's world can be hectic, ecstatic, stressful, exciting and frustrating all at the same time. We look around us and see almost every face in a crowded shopping centre full of grim determination to rush ahead and grab the next bargain; persistent advertising campaigns are thrust at us from all angles, telling us what to eat, what to wear, what to drive; we are bombarded constantly by loud noise, harsh lights and fast, busy people looking dissatisfied with their lives. When was the last time you saw someone walking through a town centre who actually looked happy?

We are taught to work hard and play hard, to strive for the perfect house, the perfect job, the perfect body, to be a perfect partner and parent. If we fail in any of these things, we can be left feeling inadequate and worthless. We become another of those stressed out, strung out and often unhappy faces, rushing around in a mad effort to become a success. Yet every now and then we meet someone who seems unaffected by the hustle and bustle of society, a person who is calm, peaceful and relaxed, someone with a soothing manner, sparkling eyes and an inner smile that speaks to us of relaxed confidence and harmony.

How can we invite that harmony into our own lives? What practical things can we do to make our lives flow more smoothly, our souls sing out with delight at simple pleasures and our troubles vanish as if by magic? Some people practise yoga or meditate, others prefer Tai Chi or holistic, new age treatments such as reflexology or acupuncture. An increasing number of people, however, are turning to the age old craft of the witch.

Throw away that dusty old image of a wart-nosed hag riding a broomstick! Let go of your fantasy ideas of witches turning ex-husbands into toads at the click of their fingers. The witches of today (also called Wiccans) are creative, magical, spiritual creatures, loving the earth and honouring the seasons.

We are men and women who harness the powers of nature to gain positive advances in the lives of others and ourselves. Harming none and always striving to make magic beneficial and for the good of all, witches have power from within, never power over. Although there are aspects of the Craft that are common to all, every Wiccan has their own path to follow within that generic structure. It is a very individual faith and what you get out of it depends very much on what you put into it. We cannot half-heartedly attend Wiccan ceremonies and expect to be immediately accepted as Wiccans, we need to have the strength of our convictions behind us. We can study, learn and practice the ways that have been put down for us and through this find the way to our own pathways and beliefs.

Finding your personal path within the sphere of Wicca and feeling at ease and content with it can take time, but once the right path has been found, we experience with it a sense of fulfilment or contentment. These feelings are common among Pagans and Wiccans who say that finding their religion or life-path felt like 'coming home'.

Contrary to other faiths, Wicca gives us the power to be our own Priestess or Priest, we are not told how to act or how to worship, except in very basic terms. Occasionally elders of the wider Pagan or Wiccan community might take matters in hand if a newcomer is acting out of order, but these instances will be very few and far between. It is one of the beauties of the Craft that we are free to practice as we see fit and are not beholden to any strict dogmatic chains that would tie us down. We are free to fly and explore for ourselves, knowing there are plenty of resources available to help us smooth our path.

Beginning with some of the most frequently asked questions, this book aims to be a springboard to your own creative and magical ability. Each chapter of the book gives ideas to get you started and you will get the most out of it by keeping an open mind and remembering that some of it may not apply to you and that is perfectly acceptable; witches are first and foremost individuals, after all. If everyone did the same things in exactly the same ways every time, the Craft would lose much of its appeal and stagnate or even die out altogether. Your own imagination, inspiration and belief are the only things you truly need to practice magic and benefit from what you are beginning to learn.

What is Paganism?

Paganism has its roots deep in our history. At its simplest, the word Pagan means 'of the country'. This is the biggest clue we have as to what our Pagan ancestors believed; they lived in harmony with the earth and used Her resources wisely, they looked to nature for divination and marked time by the change of the seasons. The old religion of our ancestors, Paganism was largely replaced in Britain by Christianity and in the mid-fifteenth century it became heresy to practice the old worship of nature deity and those caught doing so were put to trial and often hung or burned as witches. The majority of these people were the village wise-women, using their magic to heal rather than to harm. Despite the persecution of the past, the basic elements of Paganism as a nature religion have remained or have been renewed and Pagans are once again connecting to nature and the universal energy that connects and runs through all of creation.

There is no governing body of Paganism and it is hard to know how many practising Pagans there are. We do know the numbers are growing steadily, as shown by the increase in organisations, such as the Pagan Federation, the Children of Artemis and the British Druid Order. Further signs that people are turning to paganism are seen in the high street in the crystal and new-age shops, mind, body and spirit fairs, book shops with whole sections dedicated to Wicca and Paganism.

Pagans live with reverence of all nature, respect for ourselves and fellow humans, respect for all flora and fauna, connecting to the spiritual aspects of the earth, seeing the beauty in all things – the mountain or the spider.

What is Wicca?

The word Wicca is often used today as a substitute for Witchcraft. It comes from the same root word as witchcraft and means essentially the same - 'to know' or 'to bend'. Many people prefer the term Wicca to Witchcraft, as it doesn't have assigned to it the same evil connotations; the image of the wizened crone, riding a broomstick with a black cat perched on one end.

Wicca is working with universal energy for positive change and healing. Wicca is an old way of life; the traditional witch was the village wise woman who knew which herbs would heal and which would poison; they were also the shaman who could draw bad spirits away from the sick or injured, leaving them whole and healthy again.

Witches cast spells to heal and help, never to hinder or harm. Using various techniques, some of which are explored in this book, witches send positive energy out into the universe to change circumstances and bring about benefit to themselves or to others. Crystals, tarot, runes and herbs are among the tools of the craft and a witch may use all, some or none of these to cast spells.

Wicca is about celebrating life and nature and the changing cycles of the year. Witches will gather to mark the seasonal festivals and changes in human life, birth, coming of age, marriage and death.

Modern witches are in tune with the natural energies that surround and connect us all. Usually more sensitive to the energies of other people, some witches find themselves drawn to professions in which their intuitive, healing skills can be used, such as nursing, counselling, social work or care work. And yet still, we are everyday people doing both mundane and extraordinary things, we are teachers, parents, accountants, computer engineers or gardeners, among other things. Whatever skills a witch has in her daily life, be it cooking for a household of ten or planting organic vegetables, she will likely incorporate some aspect of that into her magical life and celebrations.

Do Witches Dance Around Naked?
Witches will dance, certainly, but nakedness is optional. Some solitary witches or covens may choose to work naked indoors but outdoors? Not likely in cold and windy Britain, unless you can find somewhere private enough in summer! Hence the thick cloaks and robes that some witches prefer to wear. Having something special to wear, just for ritual, gives us a sense of occasion and separates our magic from the ordinary.

Nudity in magic has two attractions, however. Traditionally, when everyone is naked, we stand as equals with nothing to mark us apart or indicate hierarchy; secondly, nudity frees us from everyday trappings and gives us greater sensitivity to subtle magical energies and auras.

Some covens prefer to be skyclad, but you will never be forced to do anything naked and if a coven or group requires this in order for you to join, you will be told beforehand and given the choice of whether or not to go ahead.

Do Witches Have Sex in Rituals?

Sexual intercourse should be a personal, private and loving act and all witches respect that. Sex is also a natural source of wild, untamed power and the energy raised during lovemaking can be harnessed for magic. Witches may choose to do that by focusing clearly during their lovemaking on what they want to achieve. This is should only be done between consenting adults, who are established partners, as part of a private ritual to raise energy and power.

What is the Great Rite?

The Great Rite is an enactment of the union between the Goddess and the God, the rite stems from the Gardnerian style of Wicca. It is a symbolic, loving, union of male/female energies without the need for nudity or sex of any kind.

To do this ritually, the Priestess will hold a chalice or goblet of water as representation of the Goddess and the Priest will put his athame into the chalice as representation of the God combining his masculine essence with the feminine essence of the Goddess. The balancing of female/male polarity is important to witches and so it is symbolised to help bring balance and polarity to our magic.

Do Witches Have Special Tools for Magic?

Witches use a variety of tools, such as crystals, the chalice, pentacles and runes but the main three are: -

The Athame – the ritual, black-handled knife. Traditionally used only for casting the circle and focusing energy. The Boline is a white-handled knife traditionally used for inscribing (candles etc) and cutting (ribbons, cords etc) during rituals.

The Wand – usually wooden, often decorated with crystals or symbols. It is used to focus energy and cast the circle if an athame is not used. Wands can also be bound with ribbons and used as a way of storing magic for release at a later date.

The Broom – the most widely recognised symbol of the witch is sometimes still used to cleanse the circle before rituals begin, sweeping away negative energy.

Do Witches Worship Any Deity?

Witches have both a God and a Goddess, although which deity is called upon in ritual will depend greatly on what the ritual is for.

Some of the most common Goddess names are Aradia, Diana, Epona, Rhiannon, Kali, Hecate, Cerridwen, Isis, Mother Earth or simply The Lady. She is the triple Goddess of the moon in her three phases of Maiden, Mother and Crone. Mother of all life, she is the female aspect of Divinity.

The God is also known by many names; Herne the Hunter, Pan, Lugh, Cernunnos, Osiris, the Green Man of the Woods, the Horned One, The Lord. He is the father of all life, protector of wild creatures, the hunter and the hunted. He is the male aspect of Divinity.

Dispelling the Fear: Do Witches Practice Satanism?

Witches do not believe in God in the Christian sense of the word and as the Devil is his opposite and comes from the same theology, we do not worship or believe in the Devil either. Witches do not sacrifice babies or animals. Anyone practising Satanism is certainly not a Witch, even if that is what they choose to call themselves. True witches work for positive goals only.

What are the Differences Between Black and White Witches?

There is no such thing as a black or white witch; there is only magic and how we choose to use it. All humans are capable of both helping and harming so we might as well ask 'Are you a good human or a bad one?' Put into that context, it seems a bit ridiculous. If you are a Witch, however, people always want to know, so on occasion, the term of White Witch can be a quick way of answering that annoying question without going into details.

Do Witches Worship the Moon?

We do not worship the moon; we respect it as a powerful symbol of the cycle of the triple Goddess. We believe that the moon has a great influence on the earth and on us and we use her cycles to aid our magic. The full moon ritual is called an Esbat and each month at this time witches gather in covens to perform magic and celebrate the cycles of life and give thanks for our gifts. The moon has many Goddesses associated with her, such as Luna, Diana, and Aradia.

Do Witches Perform Exorcisms?

Exorcism is a Christian term. What witches can do is to cleanse and purify a house or a person. We can cleanse away unwanted energy and bless a place, or indeed a person, with peace and happiness, protect it with magic and bring about a peaceful atmosphere.

What is Magic?
Magic is the art of changing consciousness at will. Put more simply, we use our will, our focus and intention, to change the material world. We harness the natural energy of the universe and direct it where it needs to go in order to bring about our goal.

Does Magic Work?
Providing it is done with focused, clear intentions and enough energy and will power is put into it, magic does work. When magic fails either it is not the appropriate time for that thing to come about, we have done it wrong, we have not been focused enough or have been wishing for harmful things that our Goddess and God will not support.

Are There Different Types of Wicca?
There are many types of Wicca being practised today ranging from the very formal to very simple. Some of the most popular styles of craft being practiced today are Gardnerian, Alexandrian, Traditional, Hereditaries, Dianic, Reclaiming Tradition, Solitary or Hedge-witchcraft and progressive witchcraft.

They all have different ways of working; some are more formal, with written scripts followed for each rite and a degree system of initiation, others are more creative, eclectic or spiritual in nature; but all retain the fundamental basis of attuning oneself to nature and the seasons, celebrating the eight festivals, using natural energy for spells and healing and connecting to the Goddess and God.

What is a Coven?

The term coven may be applied whenever any group of witches gather to celebrate the Sabbats and work magic.

The traditional number in a coven is thirteen. It has been said that this number comes from the thirteen full moons in a year, rather than the number of the group.

Although many witches do gather in groups or covens, it is increasingly common for witches to be solitary practitioners who meet only occasionally, or for each Sabbat, with larger groups of like-minded people. There are many reasons for this, the most common being work or family commitments preventing larger numbers of people all having the same date free in their busy lives. Some witches simply prefer doing ritual and magic on their own.

Do You Have to be Initiated to be a Witch?

No, although Initiation is an option you might want to consider at some stage. Some covens have three or more levels of initiation, each level giving higher status.

There is a lot of talk in witchy circles about self-initiation and if this is the same as coven initiation. My view is that a dedication ceremony can make you part of a coven but, even in a solitary ritual, your true initiation comes from the Goddess and God who accept and acknowledge us as witches.

What is the Book of Shadows?

The vast majority of witches will have a book or journal in which they write up their personal spells, recipes and journeys. This is called the Book of Shadows because a written account can only ever be a shadow of the real thing, and also because in times of persecution, a witch would have to hide away all evidence of her practice and keep very much to the shadows as she cast her spells.

There is no one 'true' or definitive Book of Shadows that all witches use or have a copy of. It is a personal thing, with each witch creating her own. A Book of Shadows can be instructional, with rituals for each Sabbat and Esbat, guidelines on how to cast a circle, perform consecrations and how to create spells. It can also be a sacred journal of your progression and experiences of magic and journeys. Every Witch writes her own journal in which she keeps her magical recipes and this will be added to over the years as she learns and progresses through the craft.

2

Ethics

Rumour has it that witches have no morals, no standards or ethics. But this is far from being true. We are no less moral or ethical than anyone else and hopefully, most witches strive to have high ideals and moral standards. Some witches choose an organic, vegetarian or vegan diet so that we do no harm to animals. As followers of a nature religion, witches also take care of the environment in many ways, including recycling, limiting car use, and choosing to cycle and walk instead, supporting organisations like Friends of the Earth or Greenpeace. Every April, witches and Pagans across Britain and many other countries celebrate World Earth Day by going on litter picks and woodland tidy-up days as part of our work in the community. Many witches will also stand up for human rights by buying fairly traded produce and donating generously to charity appeals in times of national and global crises.

In terms of being ethical in a magical sense, we have a saying in Wicca that whatever we send out returns to us three-fold. This tenet, sometimes called the boomerang effect, encourages us to think carefully and consider the implications of what we are doing, in case it rebounds upon us in ways we hadn't anticipated. If we are worried that our magic spell will bounce back and cause us harm, that worry indicates that we intend or think our spell will cause harm to someone else and we can then revise our aims to avoid that harm. Nobody who genuinely wants to cause physical or emotional harm to someone would want to have that harm come back to them, especially as that magic will affect us three times worse than it affected our intended victim.

Belief in Karma, that is, a balancing of actions and consequences that remains with us through repeated life-times, gives us good reasons to carry out good deeds; if we help someone in this life, that person may do us a good turn in the next life, whereas if we cause harm, we can expect to have that same harmful energy come back to us in the next life. It is widely believed, though not exclusively among witches, that trials and adversity we strive to overcome in the present day can be the result of Karma from previous incarnations. Instant Karma, on the other hand, suggests that any exceptionally kind or harmful action we do can occasionally be rewarded within a matter of weeks or days, for better or worse, depending on what we have done.

The ethics of Wicca can perhaps be best summed up in the following phrase, commonly known as the Wiccan Rede.

> 'Eight words the Wiccan Rede fulfil,
> An it harm none, do what thou will.'

The vast majority of Wiccans agree and hold with this statement and try to live by it as well as do magic by it. Far from giving us the freedom to go out and do whatever we want, this gives us a moral code by which we try to live our whole lives, not just our magical lives. If we go out to a party and get roaring drunk, we usually wake up with a hangover. This is harming ourselves, and whether we wanted that hangover or not, it is not fulfilling the Wiccan Rede. Most people drive a car to work each day and scientific evidence shows us that causes pollution, which in turn contributes not only to global warming but also to increased levels of childhood asthma and other health disorders, yet most people choose to drive anyway because of the benefits they receive from private transport. Of course, that takes the Wiccan Rede to extremes, but the principal remains.

If you know or suspect that your actions, both in magic and in daily activities, will cause any type of harm to others or to yourself, then you need to weigh up the cost of that action and decide if the possible benefits outweigh the harmful costs. Every time magic is done, we ask ourselves if this is going to harm anyone or anything. We try to make sure that we only do positive magic and often the last line of a spell goes along the following lines: 'If it harm none, so mote it be,' or, 'Ancient Goddess, hear my call, may this spell work for the good of all.'
There are times, however, when we may feel that somebody deserves to be punished for the harm they have caused. When we feel bitter and angry about it, our spells are likely to be ones that perpetuate a cycle of hatred and harm. Far better to get rid of our anger before we do any spells, we can then concentrate clearly on how best to deal with the situation. That might mean going to the police to report a crime and following through with magical action to make sure that justice is served and the criminal stops his activities.

This gives you the same feeling of release that you get if you throw something in the midst of an argument. For deeply seated anger, something more powerful is required; there are plenty of techniques for this, such as writing down the reason you feel so angry and burning the paper, asking for the anger to burn itself out and the Goddess and God to take the anger from you. It is recommended that magic is never done if you still feel angry; how would it feel if you cast a curse on someone you hated and they later met with a nasty accident? Ask yourself if you can really live with the consequences of your actions.

When we feel that stopping someone from doing further harm is really necessary and we have released our feelings of anger, aggression and grief, we can then work out ways of acting magically to stop them. This is called binding magic and is a way of stopping someone from doing harm without harming them in turn. There are several ways of binding someone and these will be examined later chapters.

Healing magic also has ethical dilemmas for the witch. The most caring and compassionate person does not know what is going on in someone else's mind and knowing the best way to help them involves finding out what they need and want. Working magic without the permission or knowledge of whomever the spell will help is manipulating them, however good your intentions. You may cast a spell to heal someone without asking first if you think they would not approve of magic and therefore say no to your offer of help. If this were the case, how much more would they disapprove if you went ahead and did it anyway? It is also plain rude not to ask and people who are in desperate situations can often be more open than you would think to alternative methods of healing and help.

If you don't ask permission from someone, don't just assume that they wouldn't mind; ask them if you can help, and remember that magical help does not have to be a spell, it could be visualisation or meditative prayer to the Goddess and God.

3

Creating Sacred Space

Creating sacred space is the foreplay of ritual. It is how we prepare for rituals and create an atmosphere conducive to our rites. Sacred space lets us connect to the divinity within everything and serves to separate us from the banality of our usual activities. With regular practise, setting out our sacred space becomes in itself enough of a ritual to focus our minds properly on the ritual ahead.

Sacred space is so vital to all of our rituals and practice that we are taught the techniques of creating it very early on in our explorations of Wicca. Once this basic training is out of the way, it is rarely, if ever touched upon again. People assume that once you've done it a couple of times, there is no more to learn and nothing to gain from further training in the art of creating sacred space. However, as with any skill that can be learned, we can all benefit from reviewing or even changing our techniques from time to time, recapping on our old teachings and using new methods or experimentation.

Creating sacred space is done in a wide variety of ways and in many Wiccan circles it often starts with decorating a room to make it look good and witchy – usually with plenty of incense and a wall-hanging with a pentacle painted on it. In fact, these are only the outer trappings of sacred space and the things which are the least necessary in contributing to the environment becoming sacred. Sacred space starts from within – it is through our personal preparations that we can attune ourselves to the energies of the universe.

Before we make our space sacred, we need to make sure we are ready to be in that sacred space – we need to be free of unwanted stress and negative energy, we need to ready ourselves for ritual. Several exercises can be learned which help with this and although those laid out below suggest a variety of tools to use, note well that while they help, none are absolutely necessary and can even get in the way if you focus on them too much.

Within Wicca sacred space normally means casting what we call the magic circle. Some form of cleansing or grounding will normally be done before the circle is cast and setting up an altar before you commence ensures you have everything to hand in advance, although the altar in itself is unimportant. The magic circle is a place of power and empowerment; within the circle we can call up the elements and energy we need to make magic and celebrate events. We feel ready to take on the world. This is as it should be, for we need belief and confidence in our abilities in order to truly change the way things are.

The magic circle is the temple of the Goddess and God, the sacred place where we come together to work magic, celebrate the changing seasons and perform ceremonies such as handfastings. This sacred space is created anew each time we use it. If the weather is good, we can cast a circle outdoors, using real aspects of the five elements as our altar pieces, instead of representations. If it is cold or we don't have access to a private site, rituals are done indoors, usually in somebody's lounge with the furniture pushed out of the way.

There is no right way to set up your sacred space and cast a circle; everyone has preferences and most witches are willing to try something new or unusual. That said, there are common elements to the way things are done by the majority of Wiccans. This includes setting up the altar on which to keep incense for example, personal cleansing or grounding, then casting the circle and invoking the five elements, finally calling on the Goddess and God to be present in the ritual.

The Altar

Witches have a tendency of hoarding all kinds of tools and paraphernalia to do with the craft; there are statues of the God and Goddess to collect, plus an array of candles and incenses. That's without mentioning special charms and amulets or seasonal flowers and any tools, such as the athame, wand or rattle that we might like to use. Every witch's home will have a special place set aside solely for the purpose of keeping our witchy belongings, even if it is a shoe-box tucked out of sight under the bed, away the eyes of prying visitors. The altar is where we place our tools during rituals; usually this is a small table or a special cloth spread on the floor.

If you have plenty of space, you could set up a permanent altar, which has the advantage of not needing to pack things away each time you want to use them but the disadvantage of having to dust it every now and again. Your altar might be a small shelf, the top of a book-case, a special table in a temple room if you have a lovely large house.

If you have a house full of curious children (or adults, for that matter) it might be difficult to keep things as private as you would like, in which case you need to assess how important it is that no-one else touches any of your magical items. Would you be happy for others to see or touch your rune stones or wand? If not, the idea of keeping things safely tucked out of sight becomes appealing, perhaps wrapped in a silk cloth that can be spread on the floor or table-top as an altar cloth when you take it out to cast your circles.

There are some basic things you might like to start collecting; you don't need to spend a lot of money as most can be picked up quite cheaply from discount stores or even second-hand shops, although any previously owned item will need cleansing and consecrating before you use it. Candles, incense or smudge sticks, wand, athame, rattle or drum, Goddess and God representations are some suggestions of everyday tools that would be useful; don't forget the matches. It would also be polite to have representations of each element, as we call them into the circle often enough. You can use a small amount of salt or a crystal for earth, feathers or a cloud picture for air, a winter-red leaf or miniature dragon for fire, a seashell or a chalice for water. The fifth element, spirit, is both deep within us and outside of us, surrounding us; we are the representation, or rather, the embodiment, of spirit.

There is no right and wrong concerning the altar, despite what some people would have you believe; it comes down to personal choice and taste. A cheap and garish plastic gnome would sit happily next to a beautiful hand-crafted shamanic rattle and there need be no conflict between the two. Wicca is an old religion but also one of the present day and as witches, we move with the times, mixing ancient and modern, humour and reverence.

Seasonal flowers or fruit, pictures of the beloved dead at Samhain or a corn dolly at Imbolc are also placed on the altar to mark the passage of the year. Every festival can have its symbol on our altar and, in time, you will find your own altar becomes a mini-shrine, which changes with new offerings and different things to value and make sacred for a time.

Cleansing

In order to carry out any ritual, we need to be physically and psychically prepared for it and there are many different ways to prepare ourselves. The act of cleansing is itself a form of ritual and the intention is to rid our body and mind from the physical dirt and emotional clutter we can pick up during our regular days. This can stick to our aura (we will focus on auras later on) spoiling our mood for ritual. For example, would you necessarily want the stress and tension of your rough day's arguments with work colleagues to be hanging over you while you are trying to send calm and relaxing energy to a friend taking a test?

Providing that you visualise clearly and focus your intention on removing negative energy from whatever you are cleansing, any of these methods and those you come up with yourself will all be effective.

Draw a bath scented with lavender to relax you or ginger to stimulate your senses and wake you up. As you bathe, pour the water over yourself with the intention of cleansing. A brisk shower can be useful – as the water runs off your body, visualise the tension and stress running down the plug-hole with the water. Even washing your hands under tap water can be done with the intention of cleansing away any unwanted energies.

Light some incense or a smudge bundle and wave the smoke around your body, above your head, under your feet. Let the smoke carry all the impurities, all the daily grime, away from you.

Take a feather and whisk it around in the air that immediately surrounds your body, briskly or gently move it around the whole of your body, moving away unwanted energy to leave you feeling clean.

You can also cleanse your working area using any of these methods. If you want to carry out a house-blessing or cleansing, try sprinkling salt water around the perimeter, chiming a bell or gong to use vibrations of sound to whisk away an unpleasant atmosphere and asking for the Goddess and God to restore peace and calm.

Grounding

Grounding is an everyday Wiccan term. It means connecting to earth and sky, to the universal energy of nature. We can ground ourselves before a circle to have a supply of energy running through us during ritual or we can ground afterwards, to get rid of any light-headedness that sometimes lingers.

Exercise One

One of the best-known and most commonly used grounding methods is the Tree of Life meditation and each practitioner will do this slightly differently but each way is acceptable, as with all of Wicca, there is no right way and you are free to adapt so that it suits you better or use it as laid out below. The basic principle is to put your roots down and your branches up, drawing in energy from the sky and earth and anchoring yourself to the ground and making sure that before you cast a circle, you have access to the universal energy. It seems long-winded when written down, but in practice it will only take a few minutes once you get the hang of it.

To begin this exercise, stand up straight and lift your head slightly so that your spine creates a line from the ground to the sky. Now let your thoughts drift downwards to your feet, planted firmly on the ground. Drift down further, let the whole of your senses meet in your feet and flow through them into the ground beneath you. Let your awareness go down further, through the floor and into the earth itself, past layers of topsoil, past the worms and roots and rock. Go further with your senses, reaching your roots deeper and deeper, past underground streams and caves, right down to the hot, warm core of the earth.

Imagine wrapping your roots around a big rock, anchoring you, and see that warm earth energy slowly come up your roots. As a tree root will draw up water and nutrients so this energy is nourishing you. Now feel this energy come back up your roots, through all the layers of earth and rock, past the caves and streams, up through layers of clay, and chalk, back through the topsoil and the floor. Feel it come into your feet and gently coming to the centre of your body. Feel the energy here and know that you can draw on it any time you wish.

Now take your attention further up your body, reaching your shoulders and lifting your arms high if you like. Feel your senses rising up out of your head and into the air above you. Go higher still and out of the building, above the tallest trees and into the sky, keep going up till you reach a star and let the starlight come down to mingle with your own energy and that which you brought up from the earth. Imagine the energy of the star coming down through the sky, below the trees, through the ceiling and into your arms and your head and down into your torso. Now you have lots of energy in your body connecting you to earth and sky. Let it fill each part of your body. Gradually shift your attention back to your body and gently start to move again.

The first time you do this exercise take a few moments to familiarize yourself with how it feels. If you are light-headed after doing this, you can shake your hands, shake your body and stamp your feet to get rid of any energy you don't need. Perhaps you feel invigorated and revitalized, or you might have a strong sense of connection with the earth.

Maybe you don't feel anything at all and this does not mean you have done the grounding wrong. It can simply be an indication that you don't feel energy as strongly as others or that you need to practice. When we have spent our lives focusing on the material, physical world, it can be difficult to feel the more subtle, gentle world of energy and auras.

Exercise Two

This exercise is very simple and can be used after ritual and magic to bring you back to the here and now, earthing any light-headedness or excess of buzzing energy.

Take a stone or a crystal. Anything will do from a huge and expensive piece of clear quartz to tiny lump of gravel taken from your garden. Sit with your piece of earth in your hands. Make sure you are sitting comfortably and close your eyes.

Focus on the piece of rock or crystal and see how it feels. Is it light or heavy? Cold or warm, large or small? Spend some time thinking about this piece of earth. It has been on the earth since the dawn of time and it is older than all of our ancestors. Where did you get this? From a crystal shop or your garden? Think about that solid lump of earth, the natural state of it. Even polished crystal has only been touched on the surface.

Now feel this rock in your hands, remember its connection with the earth and reach out your mind to connect with earth through this small piece of it. Sink your thoughts down and into the rock. Imagine yourself anchoring there and depositing any extra energy you don't need, let the earth take it back for reuse another time. Take some time to see how it feels to you. When you are ready, come back to the here and now, have a stretch, touch the ground, open your eyes.

Casting the Circle

The magic circle is a boundary of energy in which we perform ritual, magic and celebrations. Casting the circle is a way of focusing our whole being on what we are doing. It sets us aside from the mundane. It is a place we call 'between the worlds', creating a pathway to other realities and realms of existence.

We cast a magic circle around our working area as a means of containing the power raised within it. Once we have cleansed our working space, the circle also provides a barrier against those things that may be working against us. This does not mean malignant spirits or evil people but anything that may be unhelpful, obstructive or not contributing to our goals in some way. The circle is made of energy, like a force field, and can be seen, felt or perceived by anyone who is sensitive to energy. Although we say 'circle' it is actually spherical, going above us and below us and we need to keep this in mind as we cast it.

In a group ritual one person will usually cast the circle and all present will reinforce it with their own focus and intention and this group focus can make for a very strong circle. A solitary witch will cast in much the same way, using her own intentions and energy to build up the circle.

When casting a circle it is not necessary to memorise the words perfectly, although to begin with it might be helpful to read a script to serve as a starting place. It is more important to remember that the intention and will behind what we say gives shape to our thoughts in creating the circle. Simply saying "Welcome Earth" and "Thank you Earth" will be good enough if you clearly focus on bringing the elemental energy into the circle. Refer to the chapter on the elements to gain an understanding of how each is used in magic and why we invite the essence into the circle.

Once cast, the circle will remain in place until you choose to dismiss it, therefore all of your working tools should be within it before you start. If you do need to leave the circle but are not yet ready to close the ritual, then you can carve a doorway in the boundary, closing it behind you and repeating the process to re-enter.

As already mentioned, it is by no means a prerequisite that you use any tools or that the running order and words given here should be followed precisely. The following example is given as a starting point for the beginner and it is hoped that with practise, you will work out how to tailor this format to your own tastes. By using this is a building block, you can begin to understand why we invoke the elements and this will lead you to perfect your own way of doing it without any of the tools or pre-written text that some Wiccans follow to the letter.

What you will need

Two candles – any colour or size
Lighter or matches
Incense and holder
Goblet or dish of water
A rock or crystal
A feather
Cake or bread
A glass of water/wine/fruit juice

How to Cast the Circle

Set up your altar in the North of your space and put everything on it. You can also decorate the room and altar with seasonal flowers and colourful drapes or throws, dim the lights and play some gentle music, such as whale-song. Move any animals out of the area you are using, if possible. Wear something loose and comfortable but be careful that your candles will not burn long or flowing garments. Cleanse your space and yourself and use a grounding technique to set the universal energy flowing through you; this energy is what will create your circle.

All of the words given here are only examples to get you started. You can make up something that feels significant or relevant to you, making sure you focus clearly is the most vital element of casting and invoking. Once you have an understanding of what each element and the God and Goddess mean, the words will be more meaningful.

Starting from the North or East, walk around the perimeter of your area, pointing your index finger at the edge of it and imagine a light coming from you to form a barrier, a force-field all around you. Let this shield go above you and below. Imagine the circle forming around you as a silver or golden colour, some people like to see it as powder blue or soft pink. You will see the perfect colour for your own circle. As you walk around, say this or something similar:

I cast this circle as a sacred space, a boundary between the worlds and a container for the energy raised within it. Let this circle be cast as a place of love and joy and truth. In the name of the Goddess and God, the circle is cast.

Go to the North and pick up the rock/crystal. Hold it up in the North of your circle and state:

> *May the spirit of Earth in the North be welcome in this circle. I ask for your presence in my rite. Hail and Welcome.*

Put the rock back down and take the feather, walk with it clockwise around your circle to the East. Hold it high and say:

> *May the spirit of Air in the East, the breeze of fresh air, be welcome in this circle, I ask for your presence in my rite. Hail and Welcome.*

You can either leave the elemental representation in the relevant quarter or return it to the altar. Now walk clockwise to the altar, light the incense and take it clockwise to the South. Hold the incense up in offering and say:

> *May the spirit of Fire in the South, spirit of desire, passion, anger and love, the fire of warmth and creativity, be welcome in this circle. I invite your presence into my circle. Hail and Welcome.*

Go clockwise to the North once again and pick up the water, walking still clockwise to the West. Hold the water up and say:

> *May the spirit of Water in the West, come to the circle and stand watch over this ritual. Hail and Welcome.*

Now go back to your altar and face the centre of your circle.

Turn your face upwards and lift your hands, saying:

> *May Spirits of love and kindness be welcome in this circle, I ask for your presence in my rite. Hail and Welcome.*

Light one of the altar candles, saying as you do so:

> *I light this candle for the Goddess and ask for her presence in my ritual. She who is love and beauty, Mother of us all. Hail and Welcome.*

Light another candle and say:

> *I light this candle for the God and ask for his presence in my ritual. He who is protective and strong, Father of us all. Hail and Welcome.*

The circle is now cast and any ritual and magical work is carried out, followed by blessing of the traditional cakes and ale, or chocolate biscuits and fruit juice in many cases, have whatever you like but never eat or drink the last of anything – save some to take outside and offer to the Old Ones after you've closed the circle.

Closing the Circle

When we have prepared both a physical and psychic place in which to perform our ritual, we need to clear it away again and open the circle. We also need to give our thanks to those presences we have welcomed into our space. The circle is put away for future use in much the same way as it was created, reversing the order in which things are done, including the direction in which you walk round the circle. Deosil, or clockwise to cast and Widdershins or anti-clockwise to close.

However you choose to welcome in the elements and Deity, it is good manners to remember to say thank you and goodbye when you have finished. It is also important magically to do so; if we are rude and offend the Goddess, she may not help us when we really need her!

Stand in the North and raise your hands and say:

> *I give my thanks to the God, Father of all life, for your presence in my circle. I bid you Hail and Farewell. I give my thanks to the Goddess, Mother of all life, for your presence in my circle. I bid you Hail and Farewell.*

Face the centre and say:

> *Element of Spirit, I give my thanks for your presence in my circle. I bid you Hail and Farewell.*

Walk to the west and hold your water high saying:

> *Element of Water in the West, cleansing rain and refreshing dew, I give my thanks for your presence in this circle. I bid you Hail and Farewell.*

Put your water back in the North, walking anti-clockwise, and go to the South and collect your incense, give thanks to fire:

> *Element of Fire in the South, I offer you my thanks and bid you Hail and Farewell.*

Place the incense back on the altar and walk to the east, collect your feather, saying:

> *Element of Air in the East, I give my thanks for your presence in this circle. I bid you Hail and Farewell.*

Return to the altar and hold the stone high, this time thanking the guardians of Earth:

> *Element of Earth in the North, thank you for standing watch over my circle. I bid you Hail and Farewell.*

Put down the rock and walk anti-clockwise around your Circle, pointing your finger at the perimeter. As you walk around see all that lovely light dissipating into the earth, gently dissolving away. Say something like this:

> *The circle returns to the source of all life. May love and joy and truth remain with me. The circle is open. So mote it be.*

In some groups, it is customary to hold hands around the circle and repeat the traditional Wiccan blessing:

> '*May the circle be open, yet unbroken. May the peace of the Goddess be ever in our hearts. Merry meet and merry part and merry meet again.*'

We lift our hands high and give a joyous shout, feeling satisfied that we will meet again and be merry.

When we have finished this ritual closing of the sacred space, we can move our magical tools to a safe place and use our living room floor as usual. One ancient custom worth observing is one of thanks, we offer the remaining food and drink to the Old Ones by sprinkling on the earth outside, thus appeasing and honouring the spirits of the Earth.

4

The Tools of Wicca

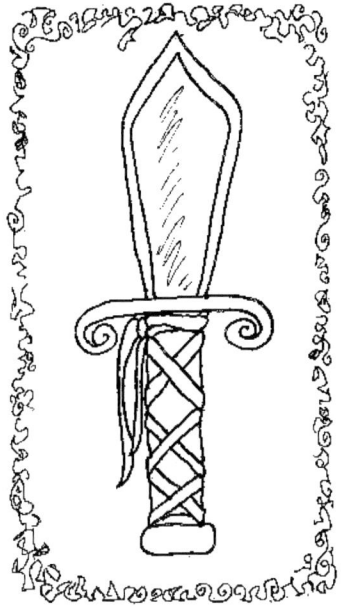

As you might have guessed, the traditional image of an old crone riding through the night sky on her twiggy broomstick is far from being truthful, yet the image persists. Witches do use broomsticks and the wand of fairy god-mother fame, although for quite different reasons than those the stories would have us believe.

There are many tools of the witch's trade, such as crystals, candles, incense, herbs, mirrors, runes and tarot cards. These are sundries, however, and can be used for cleansing, divination and spell casting among other things. Some of the more fundamental tools are the wand, athame, besom, and drums. Although there are wonderful and expensive tools available in new age or occult shops, it is not necessary to spend much on the tools, most can be picked up cheaply in second-hand or junk shops and many Wiccans make their own tools. Whether new or old, every tool should be cleansed and consecrated before use.

None of the tools have to be big and grand; take a look around your house and see if anything you already possess can be used for magic. An ordinary paper knife could be your athame and as you continue to open letters with it, do so with the wish that only good news come to you and the bills are not too high. Your wand might be a wooden spoon and you could still use it to stir up dishes and put loving magic into your cooking, affirming all those who eat at your house be blessed with happiness and peace.

The most important tool of the craft, however, is your own will power, intention and focus. No matter how much time and money is spent on making or buying tools, no magic ever worked simply by pointing a wand and shouting, 'So mote it be!' All of these tools are only an aid to magic and, with practice and concentration, all magic work can be done without them. If you are not drawn to either wand or athame and the thought of pounding drums gives you a headache, then give them away or keep them for show, but don't be tempted to use them just because everyone else does.

The Pentacle

The five pointed star, the pentagram, is called a pentacle when enclosed by a circle. The pentagram itself represents the five elements of Wicca, the human form with arms and legs outstretched and each aspect of the triple Goddess and the duality of the Horned God. The circle surrounding the pentagram represents the unending circle of life, the force of the universal All that connects everything and also the connections between each element and spirit.

The reversed pentagram, with two points uppermost, has been associated with Satanism. For Wiccans, however, the two points upwards represent the image of the Horned God and is also the symbol of the second degree initiation in Gardnerian Wicca. A large percentage of witches wear a pentagram or pentacle as some form of jewellery and usually with only one point upwards, so that it is not mistaken as a symbol of Satanism.

A pentacle can be drawn on a clay plate, a piece of wood or engraved in metal and decorated prettily with symbols and leaves. It represents the element of earth on the altar and should preferably be made of natural material. The pentacle can be a source of instant grounding and you can charge it to this effect if you desire. If you can, hand-craft one yourself with air-hardening or modelling clay or put your own design onto a circular terracotta plant holder; maybe with the flat, underneath side being decorated and placed on the altar for adornment and grounding during rituals or turned right-way up, with the depression filled with offerings or serving as a candle-holder. The choice is yours and like all of the other tools, it is not essential to have one.

The Athame

The athame, the witch's black handled ritual knife, has largely taken over from the traditional wooden wand as the most important tool of Wicca. The athame comes to witchcraft through ceremonial high magic and was kept for the sole purpose of use in ritual. Only the very rich, however, could afford to have a knife which did not serve a practical purpose and, as with the wand, if the hedge-witches of old were in possession of such a ritual knife, it served a dual purpose and was hidden amongst the ordinary house-hold items to avoid suspicion in times of persecution.

Traditionally, the athame represents fire and is used for casting the circle and directing energy. With the exception of a hand-fasting (wedding) cake, the athame is not used to actually cut anything, although it may be used to carve words or pictures into candles for spells and healing. Symbols of initiation and magical names are often carved into the handle of the knife and in some traditions, it has its own name given to it, as did the sword Excalibur of Arthurian legend; this is done to give the knife an identity of its own, making it more powerful and lending that power to magic.

The athame is used to direct and channel energy and to cast the circle. Once the circle is cast, the athame is used to cut a doorway in the boundary if you need to leave the circle before you finish your ritual. Energy can be raised through dancing, drumming or chanting and then channelled from you into the point of the athame and the athame point can then be used to charge a crystal or talisman for healing, discharging the concentrated, focused energy into the item.

A white-handled knife, called the Boline, is sometimes used for cutting things in the circle, ribbons or cords for example, though a pair of scissors can work just as well and often better.

The Wand

The wand is the wooden, natural equivalent of the athame and actually pre-dates it. Different types of tree have different meanings associated with them and this can be taken into account when choosing a wand. The witches of the middle-ages would have had a wand which doubled up as a stirring spoon or something similar, as well as being practical, this would have been a commonplace item to have around the home if the inquisitors or clergy came visiting.

Used to direct energy and cast the circle in much the same manner as the athame, the wand has other uses too. The fact that it is wooden makes it an excellent conductor of energy and magic. You can make a wand for any purpose, tying it with coloured ribbons or threads to 'store' magic for release at a later date. Decorated with runes, symbols, names or crystals, the wand is a useful tool for all kinds of magic and energy work.

Making a Wand

If you want to make a wand, rather than buying one, you might find it useful to consult a good book to explore the qualities and traits of trees that appeal to you, or maybe you will stumble across a fallen branch that seems to call out to you. A lack of firm ideas on the subject is helpful as it keeps you open to more possibilities. A closed mind with particular preferences might miss out on what would otherwise prove suitable.

Some trees which have strong associations with witchcraft include the following, though it would be advisable to do your own research, either by looking at books or talking to the spirit of the tree.

WILLOW, life-giving, the moon, visions, healing, the element of water. Willow grows very easily, especially around water. Along with its life-giving properties, willow can give insight and enhance psychic abilities.

OAK, inner strength, solidity, protection, stability, earth element, wisdom. Oak has a long history of sacred use. It is associated with the old groves of ancient druids and with mistletoe. Oak apples – round woody growths formed by trapped insects on the oak's branches – can be gently removed with the tree's permission. These are easily hollowed out to make sacred beads and can be used in rituals where great strength of character is required.

ROWAN, fire element, psychic powers, magic, protection against black magic, a Goddess tree. Rowan is also known as the mountain ash and can bring companionship to the lonely.

ASH, the element of air, clarity, intellect, balance, positive energy. Ash is a tree of power and can help in decision making or communication and legal matters.

YEW, rest, the underworld, the tree of churchyards. It is said to represent resurrection after death, connecting us with the element of spirit. Yew is a great healer, providing joy from sadness and health from sickness, used as traditional wood for runes.

Go for a walk and find a place where trees are growing strong and tall and healthy. As you walk, think about finding a piece of wood that is just right for you. Clear your mind's eye of any preconceptions of what this tree might be or what the branch might look like. Just visualise yourself picking up a piece of wood and feeling connected to it, that it is right for you.

The traditional length of the wand is from your elbow to your finger tips. You might find you are drawn to a very long, thin piece of wood or a short, chunky bit no longer than your hand. Once again, there are no hard and fast rules about what works and it always come down to individual preference.

Pick up a stem of wood that calls to you, it is preferable to take a piece of fallen wood, rather than cutting a branch from a living tree. Whatever the case, the branch should be dry, free of rot and not break easily. If you do feel drawn to cutting the branch of a living tree here are some precautions to bear in mind.

Put your hands on the tree and imagine yourself connecting with the spirit of that tree. Wait until you feel calm and still, there's no rush; if you don't feel a connection or bonding to the tree, then move on to another. Once you have made a connection with the spirit of the tree, tell it what you want and why; wait and see if you feel anything, do you get the impression that tree is saying yes, or no? Listen hard and if in doubt, take this as a lesson that you might not be ready for a wand from that particular tree and you need to either look elsewhere or wait for another occasion.

If you feel the tree will let you cut from it, take a long black ribbon or cord and ask the tree-spirit to move to the bottom of the tree. Tie the cord around the trunk so the tree-spirit will not come back up before you are finished. Now cut your branch, gently and with care; remember you are taking a branch, not performing tree surgery. Untie the cord and tell the tree spirit it can move back up if it wants to. Say thank you and leave something in exchange for your wand. This could be a nourishing drink of water or you can sprinkle some food for the birds and clear up the litter around the park.

There will still be some living energy in the wand itself, just as everything has its own energy. This is not the actual energy of the tree-spirit but a ghost of that spirit. To bring home deliberately or otherwise the true spirit of any other living being would be rude, arrogant and even dangerous. If you find the energy in your wand is still very strong or unfriendly, you should return the wood and let it go. Find another piece of wood that will be more amenable to your needs.

Take your wand home and cast a circle as soon as you get the chance. You might want to wait for a full moon and use the moon's energy to enhance your ritual experience.

While still in the circle, you can embellish the wand in any way you want; engrave the wand with symbols and runes, tie on ribbons, glue crystals on it. Make sure you have everything to hand before you start and do all of this with a sense of the sacred. Follow the guidelines for cleansing and consecration of ritual tools, make a connection between yourself and the residual energy of the tree-spirit that will still be in the wood.

The Besom

The broomstick of old, the besom, is not used for flying, this rumour probably comes from an old form of sympathetic magic, when witches, and often farmers themselves, would thrust it upright in the fields and jump high into the air. This was done to encourage the crops to grow high and strong. Other stories of witches flying come from rumours of 'flying ointment', a mixture of fat, herbs, roots and other plant matter that was rubbed into the skin to produce hallucinations. During these hallucinogenic episodes, witches would frequently report that they were flying high above the heads of those gathered and could explain in detail what had been going on and what it looked like from above, while those still on the ground would say that he or she had never left it.

The broom is an old symbol of fertility, the end of the staff is often carved into the shape of a penis and planted firmly in among the bristles of womanhood.

As well as symbolising the union of man and woman, Goddess and God, the besom is traditionally used to clean the house and this is still its main function in Wiccan circles today; sweeping widdershins around the room to get rid of both dust and negative energy before the circle is cast. It is used during hand-fasting rites, when the happy couple will jump over the besom, wishing for fertility and a happy life together. Any other couples who want to secure their relationship will follow the bride and groom in jumping over the besom, usually held a foot or so above the ground.

There are many places to buy besoms from, especially around Samhain, but most of these are poor quality and not very durable. A magical broom should be built to last – it may actually get used, after all, year in and year out. Some parts of the country run rural craft workshops, making anything from rustic furniture to decorative ornaments and it is likely that you will be able to find one for besom making if you are feeling up to the task.

Drums and Rattles

Many different drums can be used in ritual and have two purposes; to provide a background beat for dancing and raising energy; as an aid to journey work, firstly with a steady rhythm as the journey is undertaken and secondly with a pounding, non-rhythmic and much faster drumming as a call-back from journey. For dancing and raising energy, the hard, fast tempo of large, African djembes are popular, whereas for journey it is more common to use the circular, hand-held Irish bodhran, played with a rhythmic thumping beat.

Rattles can be used to cleanse the body, the aura and the space you are working in. By shaking a rattle and asking for the space or aura to be cleansed and free of negativity, you send out vibrations to dislodge any unpleasant atmosphere or unwanted emotions before doing magic. This could even be done as a ritual on its own, to carry out a house-cleansing for example. The rattle can also be used for the same purposes as the drum, although it is not so effective for journey work.

Cleansing the Ritual Tools

If you decide to use any ritual tools, they will need to be cleansed of any previous energy they have collected, even if bought new, as everything has an aura, not only people and animals. Cleansing can be done by covering the tool in sea-salt for twenty-four hours, holding in running water for a few minutes and visualising all the energy draining away or by using a smudge bundle or incense smoke to literally 'smoke-out' the energy. Whatever method you choose to cleanse your tool, it is your own intention which carries out the cleansing and it can be done by simply visualising it. Even if you decide against having any ritual tools, here's an exercise you can try with any object you have lying around you as a way of raising your awareness of energy and auras.

Holding the tool in your hands, close your eyes. Spend a short while trying to sense the energy of the tool. Does it feel cold, warm, hard or spiky? Run your hands over it and get used to its weight and touch.

Now hold it one hand and take the other a foot or so above it. Bring your hand slowly towards the object and see if you can sense when you are touching its aura. Gently move your hands about and visualise yourself pulling away anything that feels wrong or bad, shift away everything that you don't want there, move it with your hands, pick bits off with your fingers or simply hold the object in both hands and reach out with your mind to cleanse it. See all the energy you remove drifting away and ask that it be returned to the earth to be recycled. Ask that all negative energy from this item is restored to the source of universal energy so that it can be neutralised and used again. Imagine it sinking into the deep earth or flowing out on airwaves of energy, far away from you. When you feel that the aura of the object is clean or neutral, come away from it for a moment and shake your hands gently to release energy and distance yourself from the item.

Now try again to feel the energy and see if it is any different, make sure you really do feel like this is a clean and purified object, a blank canvas ready to use in the circle or to be charged with magic.

Consecration

Consecration is a way of dedicating our tools to the sole purpose of ritual and magic and to bless them with each of the elements and the Goddess and God. Consecration can be done for anything you wish to bring into the circle, candlesticks, special jewellery, robes or crystals.

Make your sacred space comfortable and luxurious by decorating the altar, hanging pictures up and placing soft throws on the floor to sit and walk upon. Elaborate and use your imagination; as you create sacred spaces, remember you are the one who has to use it so make it as beautiful or plain as your tastes allow, make it a space that relaxes you and makes you feel at home. Put all of your ritual items on the altar along with the new tool you are going to consecrate.

Cast your circle, imagining the sphere of energy like a cocoon to keep you warm and safe. Invoke the essence of each element and the Goddess and God to be present. Try to have a representation of each element on your altar, a cup of water or a sea-shell for water, a dish of soil or a crystal for earth, a feather or some incense for air, a swatch of red ribbon or a candle for fire. Spirit, as always, is both within you and outside of you, although it can be represented by a pentacle placed in the centre of the altar.

Hold up your tool to the North or touch it to the ground if you are outdoors. Focus on earth and its connection to your tool and to you and say:

> *I consecrate this athame/wand with the element of Earth, may it be blessed with Earth's qualities of stability, comfort and firmness. I do this that it shall serve me as an aid to ritual and magic. So mote it be.*

Repeat this with each element, using your own words and focusing each time on your connection to the element and what qualities you want to associate your tool with.

Move to the centre of your Circle. Hold it to your chest, feel the tool becoming tuned in to you and your energy. Now hold it up high and say:

> *Triple Goddess of the Moon, I ask that you bless and consecrate this athame/wand as a sacred tool for use in ritual. Bestow upon me the ability to use it only for good and positive goals. May this tool be imbued with natural and positive energy and always work for the good of all. As I do will, so mote it be.*

Now do this again in the name of the Horned God or use whichever Goddess and God names appeal to you and once again, think of what you want to use the tool for and ask for those qualities to come to you in this ritual.

Spend some time sitting with and getting used to the new ritual tool. Reflect on your reasons for choosing this specific style of athame, why this wood for your wand and not another? Hold it close to you and feel your aura starting to mix with that of the tool, this will become more apparent the longer you handle and use it. Think of where it will be kept when not in use and if appropriate also consecrate some soft material to wrap it with.

Without getting too broody and serious about it, this is the time to connect with the tool and ask it questions. It may sound ludicrous to ask questions of your tools as though you were having a conversation with a person, but remember that you are doing this in sacred space, a place that is between the worlds. Everything has an energy of its own and the sooner we start to accept this and deal with it, the better. So talk to your rock, your wand or athame, even your broom, and ask it if there is anything it will be particularly useful for. Ask if it has a name or if you can give it a name. Once you learn about your tools in this way, it will help you use them in the way that will prove to be most beneficial.

When you have finished communing with your new tool, bless some food and drink in the name of the Goddess and God and have some of each, keeping a little back for the Old Ones, for the fairies and for the birds.

Close the circle, saying thank you to the Goddess and God and each element in turn. This time, when you walk round the circle, use your athame or wand to dissipate the energy. Point it at the edge of the boundary and visualise the circle going back to the ground or out into the cosmos to rejoin the universal energy.

Next time you come to cast a circle you can do so using your new wand or wearing your freshly consecrated pentacle ring. If possible, newly consecrated objects should be kept as close to you as possible for at least a full cycle of the moon, in order to strengthen the connection between you and your working tools. You could keep things under your pillow, in your pockets, carry it around with you, fondle it and get used to it. You might even find you end up knowing instinctively if you lose it or if someone else is touching it without your permission.

General Wiccan etiquette dictates that it is extreme bad manners to touch or handle one another's magical tools without first asking (and receiving) permission. The reason for this is simply that we put a lot of focus into making or purchasing our tools, more energy into consecrating and cleansing them, yet more still to attune them to our personal energy and magical work, plus all the hours spent in rituals and spell crafting building up a relationship with the tool. If another person were to handle your wand, they might unknowingly leave traces of their aura and workings with it and you would have to cleanse and re-attune it to yourself a second time.

From time to time craft tools are handed down from one Wiccan to another, either by inheritance or as a gift, and each of these magical gifts come with a long history and we can never know the full working life of the newly acquired tool. For such occasions, it would be advisable to accept graciously and find out as much as you can about the uses to which the tool has been put so that you can cleanse away anything you are not comfortable with. It is highly likely, however, that the person presenting the gift is someone you know and trust very well and have probably been working magically with for some time and, in that case, you would already know the working history of the tool. Cleansing gifted tools is a matter of personal choice; on the one hand you might want a fresh start and to consecrate the tool specifically for your use, on the other hand, it will eventually become attuned to you through use anyway and it could prove useful to have the lingering energy of someone you love and respect working with you for positive goals.

The Wiccan tools, then, are a personal extension of your aura and magical energy. They become attuned to us and can be used to direct energy and focus intent. A wand or athame can be bound with ribbons or cords used in spell workings as a way of contributing energy to that spell even after we have released the energy for it into the universe. A Tibetan singing bowl can be our magical instrument, used to call up the element of air and aid communication magic by sending strong vibrations to those who need to speak up for themselves. We might use the besom inherited from our grandmother to clean our circle area before working, thereby adding Grannie's warmth and love to our celebrations and rituals.

Tools can add much to our Wiccan life, even if all they give us is something for our eyes to rest on as we look at the altar. Remember though, that no matter how grand and well-loved the tool, all the tools in the world cannot make magic by themselves and the greatest of Wiccans and healers need nothing more than themselves to bend the universe. Feel proud of yourself for creating your own set of tools to use and feel equally proud of yourself if you choose to use nothing more than your fingertips, your voice, your heart and your mind.

The Tool of You

The most important tools of all are your own mind and body. Your body contains your own energy and acts as a conductor for the external energy used in ritual and magic. It is very good at its job too, as you will experience as you carry out later exercises! It is really easy to use yourself as a magical tool. You are already filled up with energy for starters. Another useful thing about using your body as a tool is that you know exactly how your body moves and feels – what it likes, what it finds hard or easy to accomplish. Your willpower, your mind, can tell your body exactly what to do and your body responds accordingly. This is an important point which we will touch on in a moment.

Fingers are of vital importance to Wiccans but sadly, they are often overlooked in favour of wands and athames. They bend in just the right way, they are warm and familiar. Fingers are very sensitive and with them you can learn how to feel energy, how to shape it and direct it. Instead of pointing a wand to cast a circle, point your fingers. If you have fingers – and you only need one to be able to point – you will never need another magical tool in your life.

Hands can be used to raise energy, to form it into the shape of an etheric, mythical Pegasus who will carry your desire into the heavens. Your hands can also join with the hands of others and together you can send a current of energy round a circle and then raise this energy up to be released for a healing ritual. Hands can be held as a comfort to someone in distress and they can spread soothing, blessed, massage oil to ease aches and pains.

Your voice is also important. Everyone can sing – even if you sing badly you can still do it and in a chorus of twenty other witches who are also out of tune nobody would notice even if you were a soprano so stop worrying about it and start chanting. Perhaps you are a natural poet, in which case your vocal tool can be a moving invocation to the Gods.

All of the tools in the world, however, even the tool that you are, cannot help you to improve your life, by magic or other means, if you are lacking in will-power. A good amount of will-power is of incredible significance to making magical and practical changes every day of our lives. Try to bend a spoon by following the instructions below and you should begin to see what I'm getting at here.

Have you ever tried to bend a metal spoon with your mind alone – think you can't do it? Of course you can! Go to your kitchen right now and take an ordinary metal dessert spoon, nothing too heavy or cast in iron. You are now going to bend that spoon using your will-power alone; you can do it!

Take your spoon in both hands. Now begin to apply some physical pressure with your hands at the point where the spoon joins its handle. It should soon start to bend, just keep putting on that pressure, physically bend the spoon. Done it? Of course you have! All with the power of your best tool – your mind. You might call this cheating but because we are not all Uri Geller we have to be more practical; but it was still your mind and your desire to get it done that achieved the result – you started a chain reaction of chemical impulses in your brain and body that let you bend the spoon. Your mind is an all mighty force to be reckoned with and the sooner you agree with this and start believing in yourself, the sooner you will be able to work magic, conjure energy and transform your life.

5

Energy Work and the Cone of Power

Energy work means different things to different people. Reiki masters use their hands to channel universal energy for healing and balancing. Chi Quong practitioners use a series of gentle movements to calm and harmonise their own energies and bring themselves a peaceful state of being. As Wiccans, we can use energy for healing, spell-craft, empowerment, charging and consecration of tools or creating thought-forms. The cone of power is a specific way of gathering and channelling energy to release for spells during rituals.

Working with energy is the very life-breath of Wiccan practice. Energy itself is neither negative nor positive, light nor dark. Universal energy is the most commonly used and also the most generic form. This energy runs through everything, living or inanimate. It exists both within us and without. We can gather it up by reaching out with our hands and plucking it from the Web of Life, by dancing and chanting, through sex magic or other techniques, some of which we will examine here.

There are other sources of energy, earth energy, fire or water energy for example, in addition to the universal source. These alternative sources are equally natural and can be much more appropriate to our specific magical goals than the very broad and widely used universal energy.

All the energy we use in rituals and magic making should be exogenic, never our own internal energy; although we can be left exhausted or light-headed after ritual, it is our physical exertions and the sensations of energy coursing through us that causes these side-effects. Grounding is often done before rituals to try and avoid or limit the affects of magic. It provides a direct line to the limitless source of natural, universal energy to use in our magic and our own energy reserves are not depleted quite so much. If we have that running source of energy already in place, we can connect to it immediately after ritual to feel human again more or less instantly.

Using energy effectively comes only through practise and must be preceded by first learning how to sense and handle it. This comes more easily to some people than it does to others, but you should not let this deter you as it is commonly held that everyone can sense and use energy to some degree, even if it takes a lot of trial and error to find your feet. It is easier to learn about your own energy before moving onto the external sources and the aura is the ideal place to start doing this.

The Aura

The aura is the astral body which surrounds the physical one, it extends above and below us as well as in every direction outwards. It is usually seen as layers of varying colours and if you stretch your arms to their full length away from your body in any direction, that is about the area to which the aura will normally extend.

The aura can be seen in different colours and everyone's aura will be different colours at different times. What seems like a big black blob of anger in a person's aura might be an indication of physical illness or disease. Red or gold might indicate that person is feeling fired up about something and blue could represent sadness. Individual interpretations will always vary – if you see a particular colour, rely on your instincts to find out what that colour means when you see it.

Our aura can be affected by many things; our moods, the general atmosphere we are working or living in, the seasons and weather, illness or depression. It can also alter through the actions of others. For example, the person sitting next to you in a busy waiting room somehow seems to intrude on your personal space. Maybe you had a bad day at work or argued with your partner. All of these things, by themselves or as an accumulated effect, can make us feel invaded, unclean or angry and these feelings can often linger after the event itself has left our conscious mind, making them seem inexplicable. Just as you will find particles of sand in your shoes several days after you walked on the beach, so you can find particles of negative energy in your aura that don't belong there.

We get rid of anything that doesn't belong to our aura by carrying out one or more cleansing exercises. These will also prepare us for rituals, making sure that although we may remember the event, we are not dragging the atmosphere and unpleasantness of it into our sacred space. You could still do a ritual and there is a possibility that spells might still work, but it would be like baking a cake without first washing your hands and utensils – guaranteed to spread bacteria; you don't want your psychic dirt affecting your intended result, so like washing your hands for baking, you need to clean your aura for ritual.

Sensing and cleansing the aura of inanimate objects is not dissimilar to that of living beings, although 'live' auras are more difficult to interpret. To sense this life energy in some way is a skill, which like any other requires practice. You have already seen how the aura of your tools can be sensed and hopefully you have felt it too. However, to do this regularly with any degree of success does take a bit of practice and it should be pointed out that seeing, rather than feeling, the auras and energies are quite different experiences. Practice is the only way to gain confidence and skill in aura sensing and some people might never achieve it at all, so do not feel too disheartened if you aren't able to do it at this early stage.

One easy way to see your own aura (almost fail-proof) is to sit in a dark room with a single candle lit in front of you. Put your hands around the candle, with your hands on the other side of the candle to your body. Have your fingertips touching and both palms facing you. As your eyes adjust to the light, stare at your fingers and slowly draw them slightly apart and touch them together again several times. Look at the space between your fingertips and you should be able to see your aura between them. The aura may appear to be a flickering colour or a shimmering shape. This might be an almost imperceptible aura, like a piece of cling film being stretched between the fingers and as you move the hands around, the aura will move too. It might look more like a shadow or field of colour. Play with this, see how it looks with your fingers spread wide apart or very close together. Find a partner and each put one hand behind the candle to see how it looks when your different auras touch.

Another way to see the aura is to work with another person and take it in turns to stand against a plain background, black or dark colours tend to work best. Have your partner standing still and gaze at the edges of their body, around the head especially. Gradually shift your gaze to stare just a little bit away from their body and with practice you should be able to see their energy field standing out as a thick band of colour or colours surrounding them.

To feel the energy of your aura, rub your hands together very briskly, palms facing each other, as if warming them on a cold day. Now move your hands apart, about 50cm or so, and bring them slowly back together again. As you do this you should feel as though your hands are closing in on something, like an invisible ball or a force-field. Closing your eyes may help as you are not then hampered by the mind, which will tell you there is nothing there simply because you can't see it. Try this exercise with a partner and walk towards each other, palms facing your partner's palms and feel the other person's energy. You should soon be able to walk towards them and feel their aura without doing the energy raising palm-rub first. You can even try to project your aura further away from you or draw it in close and see if your partner can accurately pick up on where you are trying to project the edge of it to. If you are working alone, you can still do these exercises by trying to sense when your aura meets that of a living object, such as a tree, house plant or pet (your pet will let you know if it doesn't like this exercise by moving swiftly away, in which case you should leave it alone).

Aura Cleansing

Having found out how to sense your aura, you will be able to quickly recognise times when you have picked up negative energy and carry out some form of cleansing in the same way as described before starting a ritual. Even if you are unable to sense your aura, there may be times when you just feel wrong inside or unsettled and can't put your finger on the reason why. Carry out aura cleansing and you will most likely find that the problem has gone away or been significantly reduced.

Using the cleansing techniques from chapter three, cleanse your aura with the intention of removing unwanted energy and leave yourself feeling fresh and revived.

Use smudging, feathers or bells to cleanse the aura or use your hands again to gently shift the negative energy out of your area, picking it out with your fingers and shaking it towards the ground. Liquid, such as rose or lavender water, can also be used to cleanse the aura, so can colours or the breath. Visualise any energy you remove going along the web of life to be reabsorbed into the universal energy, or shake it towards the ground and let the earth swallow it to be recycled.

Aura Protection

Once the aura is rid of the influences of any negative energy you should feel better immediately and you can now work on protecting the aura from attracting any more undue attention. Protecting the aura can be done at any time and is especially useful if you are feeling anxious, unhappy or threatened. Not only does regular aura protection help to keep you calm and comfortable, it can also help protect you from things you aren't aware of or cannot avoid, such as nightmares when sleeping.

One proviso worth noting here is that you should make sure your aura is 'clean' before doing this kind of protection work. It would be counteractive to lock the aura against external forces if in the process you seal it up without ensuring that nothing harmful is already present.

To carry out a simple aura protection, first sit comfortably and take a few deep, regulating breaths. Relax yourself, this time by using another technique. Imagine you are lying down on a beach, neither cold nor warm, just comfortable. Your feet point to the sea and the calm, gentle waves begin to wash very slowly and soothingly over your feet then retreat again, taking with them all tension. The waves come again, this time up to your ankles or calves, softly dragging all tension away and into the sea. Picture the waves comfortably pulling away all your tensions and fears and leaving them in the sea as they retreat. As the waves reach your head, know that they are helpful and leave you completely relaxed. Let the last wave flow away and be aware of a deep sense of contentment.
Picture the aura as a hazy colour around you and concentrate on bringing more energy into your body and aura through the process of breathing in energy and exhaling it into the aura.

Mentally draw energy up from the ground and down from the sky to join your own energy. Keep up this breathing and drawing in of energy until you feel full of it. Now use your hands to direct it or mentally project some of that energy to form a solid shield around the edges of your aura, above and below you, to each side, front and back. Visualise the energy forming a barrier of silver, gold or white light through which only good may pass. State this aloud or mentally, imagining your aura working like a filter that blocks negativity while letting you absorb anything beneficial, or like a mirror which reflects away bad vibes and shines brightly to attract harmony and joy.

> *My aura is sealed against all negativity, only good and positive energy can pass through to me and I project only positive energy out to others.*

The actual words are less important than your intention to create the shield around your aura as a protective sphere and the exercise itself can be experimented with to see what colours and images work best for you. Perhaps imagining a piece of invisible gauze as your barrier will be your way of protection, or if you need an especially strong protection for some reason you can picture the shield as just that – a battle-shield that completely surrounds and protects you. Work with whatever feels right for you and go with your intuition.

Spend as long as you like building up this mental image of the aura, making it strong. With practice this will become much easier and can be done either as a daily protection or instantly in a psychic emergency when you feel threatened. Take it in turns with a partner to see if the aura can be more easily or strongly recognised when the protection is in place.

One word of caution before carrying out this aura protection exercise; make sure the aura has been cleansed first or you will simply be sealing in and carrying with you any negative influences you are striving to protect yourself from in the first place.

Chakras

Another way of making sure we are fully prepared for rituals and magic is opening the Chakras. Although Eastern in origin, the chakra system is increasingly used by Western mystery traditions, including Wicca. There are different ways of describing and defining the chakra system, the most commonly used has seven chakras, seated within the body.

These seven energy centres are a way of perceiving and regulating the flow and quality of energy. The chakras are coloured balls or wheels of energy, each one relevant to the place it sits within the body's energy system.

> Root or Base Chakra – red, represents the material world, our physicality, connects us to the earth. The root chakra is located at the very base of the spine.
>
> Sacral Chakra – orange, associated with water and positioned in the genital area, it represents our sexual and creative energy.
>
> Solar Plexus Chakra – yellow, just above the navel, this chakra is connected with fire and represents our personality, our power and will.
>
> Heart Chakra – green, located in the heart region, symbolising love, emotions and compassion, connects us with air.
>
> Throat Chakra – blue, located in the throat, thus representing communication, speech, expression.

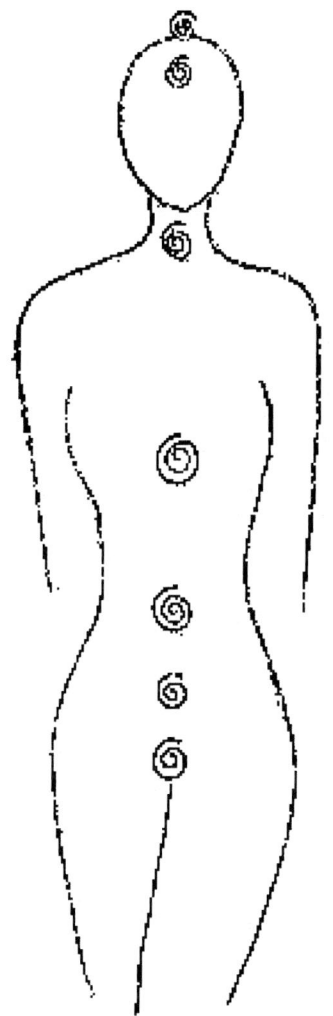

Third Eye Chakra – violet, located in the region of the brow or third eye, it is related to psychic perception, intuition, ruler of the mind.

Crown Chakra – white, the uppermost chakra is located at the very top of the head, it denotes our spiritual consciousness, our connection to the universe and the divine.

Opening the Chakras

Opening the chakras is regularly done before any ritual and will serve to strengthen routine exercises like cleansing and grounding and can also enhance your intuition and psychic antennae during ritual and magic, making you become more aware of and able to manipulate the subtle energies involved in Wiccan rituals and spell castings. Opening the chakras takes a little practice but is worth doing, as we gain an understanding of how energy flows and what it feels like. If we want to work effective magic and send energy to others for healing, we first need to be able to control our own energies and opening the chakras is one way of doing this.

Build up a picture of each chakra as a spinning vortex or swirling energy ball sitting within your body, centralised along a thread which spirals up from your feet (when standing) to the crown of your head, connecting one chakra to the next.

Stand or sit comfortably and imagine your red root chakra as a constantly moving ball of energy, swirling round and round. Imagine a thread coming from the earth leading up into the chakra.

Focus clearly on the energy of your Root chakra. See it as red, a sparkling, pulsing energy, getting bigger and more powerful the more you focus on it. Try breathing deeply, breathing energy into the chakra with each breath. Feel the root chakra become stronger until it is begins to spiral upwards along the thread to the next chakra.

Picture the energy flowing from the root and into your Sacral chakra next. An orange vortex of energy, gradually spinning faster and growing bigger, sending the limitless energy up to the next level.

Your Solar Plexus chakra, yellow and vibrant, begins to enlarge next, swelling and spiralling. See the energy coming up through the root and sacral chakras, expanding the yellow vortex and making it grow and then pass energy up along the spiral thread to the next chakra.

The green Heart chakra begins to expand now, energy still coming up from the lower chakras. See it growing bigger and stronger and try to feel the energy as it surges upwards.

Your Throat chakra now fills up and becomes a spinning, swirling ball of blue energy, growing and energising you, it fills up to capacity and energy begins to go up the thread again.

The lower chakras are still sending more energy up along the central thread, feeding your Third Eye, or brow, chakra. This violet light of the brow centre grows and spirals, larger and brighter and gives energy up to the next chakra.

As your energy spirals up to the Crown chakra, right on top of your head, visualise all the colours of each chakra coming up through the white chakra at your crown, whooshing out above you and then cascading down around you to bathe and fill up your aura.

Closing the Chakras
If we have opened our chakras in preparation to ritual and magic, we must then close them afterwards. Closing the chakras is done in reverse, from the top down and can be done more easily than opening them.

Think of the white energy that is the crown chakra, visualise that energy gathering around you and coming down through your crown, see the white crown chakra closing at the top, imagine the white light draping and folding around the energy centre of the chakra to close it and then flowing down the spiralling thread to the third-eye chakra. Repeat this process of closing the chakra in turn through each chakra. When you come to the root chakra, keep the spinning wheel of energy going round, however, and do not close it down as you did with the others. The root chakra is always left open as it connects our psychic and physical selves to the energy we need in our daily lives.

The Web of Life
When we work magic, we tap into the universal source of natural energy and draw upon it. We raise it, shape it, give it definition and then release it back to the source. Opening the chakras, grounding and aura sensing are all ways of connecting with and opening ourselves up to the energy we use in spell casting.

To understand where this energy goes to and comes from, we can imagine it as a web. A spider makes its web to catch flying insects and then it retreats to sit on the edge, waiting for the telltale vibrations of struggling prey. Every part of the web is connected to every other part, each strand meets countless others on its journey to the centre and the vibrations on a single strand create a ripple-effect that flows through the whole web, alerting the spider. The universal energy system works in much the same way, with everyone and everything being connected by unseen energy strands that flow through us all. We call this the web of life or Wyrd.

Spiders create beautiful webs in trees and bushes, on the underneath of disused bus-shelters, high up in ceiling corners, in fact, a spider can make its web in any place that is left undisturbed by humans and other animals for any period of time. The energy of Wyrd is likewise everywhere, all around us at all times. When we work magic, we are sending our wishes and spells out along the web, creating a ripple effect that will vibrate along the strands and jolt people into action or create a chain of events that brings our magic back to us in the form of achieved desires.

Web of Life Visualisation

To visualise the web of life, the following exercise is suggested. There is no need to cast a circle or create sacred space for this, although you could if you wanted to. Make sure you will not be disturbed for fifteen to twenty minutes and find somewhere comfortable to lie or sit down.

Rest comfortably and close your eyes. Breathe normally and relax by clenching and then relaxing all of your muscles in turn – your eyes, scrunch them tight and then release them – your jaw and mouth, tense and release. Repeat this clenching and releasing all the way down your body – arms, torso, buttocks, legs, toes.

Imagine you are standing in the middle of space, far away from planets or stars, all you can see are distant twinkling lights. You are safe, breathing comfortably and feeling strong. Be aware of your body in this deep-space place, be aware of your heart, beating strongly in your chest, powerfully beating and keeping you alive. Now imagine that a strand or thread leads from your chest outwards in front of you and behind you. Feel that as your heart beats it sends a tiny, strong pulse along the thread. Follow that pulse, see the thread swell as your heart beat flows along it, visualise it as a little bump travelling along the thread, the strand of your life.

Watch it closely and see it connect with other threads up ahead which criss-cross your thread. As your pulse reaches the other threads, it sends another pulse along each of these and now you have several pulses flowing along various strands. Follow one of these pulses, see it as blue or gold or orange, whatever colour appeals to you. See that pulse reach more criss-crossing threads as it travels along the thread.

Bring your attention back to the place in your chest where the thread passes through you and imagine that there is not only one thread but many and that these fine strands all have the strong pulsing colours travelling along them. These are not just beats going out but also beats coming to you; the energy you send out coming back to you on the web.

Now look up to see the criss-crossing strands meeting each other, all filled with tiny, coloured, pulses gliding along them. See how they form a web and visualise that at every junction the threads meet not just horizontally but vertically and diagonally as well.

Realise that every junction represents another person, animal, place or thing. Just as the junction where the threads pass through is the place on the web you are currently standing in. Look farther out into the web and see that it is endless, with millions of strands and billions of pulses.

Bring your awareness back to your body, anchored firmly in the web of life. Feel your heart beating again and become aware of your breathing.

Breathe deeply a few times and become aware of yourself physically. When you feel ready, wiggle your toes, open your eyes and return to the present. The web of life is one way of visualising the connections between us and the rest of the universe. When we raise a cone of power during rituals and magic, we can imagine the released energy racing along the strands of the web, making the appropriate connections and sparking off a chain of events that will bring about whatever we are working for.

The Cone of Power

Wicca is often called a mystery religion, but what are the mysteries? Aspiring to become more at ease with ourselves and life in general through exercises that protect and cleanse us is all very well but in a book about Wicca you expect to learn something of the mysteries, the things that people either exclude from or only allude to in their books. The problem is that the mysteries can never be learned through reading books or talking with people and attending lectures at mind, body and spirit fairs, no matter how hard you listen or how many questions you ask. The true mysteries are things which can only be experienced, like the feeling of satisfaction gained through deep journeys to meet with the ancestors or the flow of energy buzzing through you during an important ritual.

One of the most important mysteries for working magic is the cone of power. This is a swirling vortex of energy created during rituals and released into the universe to bring about material results. It is called a cone of power because that is the shape the energy raised automatically takes (an upside-down cone, that is, with the point at the top of the circle). The more people contributing to the raising of this power, the better, although a cone of power raised by one person can be just effective as that raised by a full coven of thirteen.

A cone of power can be raised for just about any purpose and does not require the use of any ritual tools; although the athame or wand may be used to direct the energy upwards at the point of release, the tool is an accessory and raised hands work just as well, especially as most people will raise their hands up automatically anyway as the cone reaches its peak. Whatever the reasons for casting magic with a cone of power the same steps are taken each time.

Let us suppose that a woman, Mary, has an important interview coming up. She will need to be confident during the event and will also want the outcome to be successful. Think of some suitable words and put these into a chant form. It doesn't have to be poetic and should contain one or two key words that can be repeated on their own over and over again. Make sure that the chant is worded in the present tense.

> *Mary is confident, Mary is strong,*
> *Mary has the job, Mary has success*
> *Mary has the job she has wanted for so long.*

The key words from this chant would be Mary, confident, job and success. Picture Mary smiling and pleased as she announces that she is about to start her new job. Now take this picture of her and, in a properly cast circle, perhaps with a background tape of lively drumming or wordless new-age music, begin to dance. Start the chant and keep in mind all the time that Mary already has the job, she just doesn't know it yet. Be positive, concentrate not on her interview, but on the success and happiness she will get when she is offered the position. Focus on her clearly and turn your belief that magic will work into a solid knowledge that it will work.

You can't raise energy if you don't move or vibrate in some way; this is not a funeral dirge and Wicca is never a dreary or dull religion. The more energy we put into our cone of power, the more powerful and hence the more likely to achieve results the cone will be. Dance wildly and free, celebrate the picture of Mary looking happy and confident, shake rattles, bang drums, clap your hands and howl and shout the chant. Before long, the power begins to make itself known as a sensation of buzzing or heat or heady awareness of the energy. Start to use your hands, athame or wand to feel where this energy is, how high, how conical, how vibrant. Carry on chanting and dancing and feeling the energy until you sense that it is growing tall and strong and beginning to form the cone shaped apex. If you start to muddle the words as you chant then start calling out the key words, which are easier to remember than the whole chant.

The energy will soon become electrifying and your hands should feel it gathering and writhing around at the top of the cone. Become aware of this and chant loudly a few times and wait until you feel the energy has reached its peak then cry out and release the power by visualising it bursting out of cone's apex. See it rushing along the strands of the web of life or zooming through space to reach its goal.

Let go of the image you held throughout raising the cone of power and take your time to come back to the here and now.
After releasing the energy, most people feel a sense of exhaustion and exhilaration and at this point you should sit down with the palms of your hands on the ground and begin to steady yourself, gradually slowing your breathing to a normal rate and letting any excess energy drain down through your palms into the earth below you. If you feel light-headed or spaced-out then begin to reach down and feel your energy meeting with the earth energy, visualise it reaching a solid boulder or tree root to anchor you back on the material plane. If it helps, touch the pentacle on your altar or hold a piece of rock or crystal. Things will feel normal again within a couple of minutes.

Have something to eat and drink, saving a little aside for the Old Ones. If you are lucky enough to have someone to work with, you can talk about it afterwards and this too can be a good way of grounding after rituals. If not, writing it down on a piece of paper or in a Book of Shadows is another good way of keeping track of your experiences and progress.

The Pudding of Power and How to Avoid it

There comes a time in a witch's life when you begin to attend group rituals, either at an open event, like a camp or conference, or as part of a closed, private coven. Most of the time these events go off without a hitch but every now and then you come across the disaster of the Pudding of Power.

The aim of energy raising is just that – to raise energy. When we mention the word 'cone', it is because the energy naturally spirals up into a cone shape. Things don't always go according to plan however, especially if you are working on Pagan-Meantime. People may be late, forget their tools, forget which element they are supposed to be invoking or arrive hot and flustered because they were too busy getting ready to take a few minutes out of their schedule to focus on the intention of the ritual. All of these factors can contribute to a shaky, unbalanced energy and this in turn can lead to the pudding of power.

Imagine a dozen witches all trying to raising energy by clapping and chanting and stomping around the circle. Some of them will be singing out of tune, others have no sense of timing. Drumming, no matter how enthusiastically it is done, needs to be done in a controlled manner or the drummers can easily get swept up with the beat and become out of sync with everyone else. As well as being in their own head-space and aware of their own energy levels, people have to remain aware of and connected to the group energy. It can get a little hectic and unfocused. As the energy begins to rise one or two people (and these people are not always the novice members) will think 'here it is!' and try to release the energy which they have brought to the circle. Meanwhile, across the circle from them is someone else who thinks 'this energy is not ready yet'. This person will keep their energy low and continue to work on building it as the other person is trying to release it.

As you might guess, this tends to result in a floppy, up and downy, energy mass, which is neither collapsing entirely, nor being raised to the height or mass required for a cone of power. It is more like a squashed dome or pudding shape, than the cone that is really needed to result in manifesting the desired outcome. Unfortunately, the pudding of power is often released at this stage if there is no-one present with enough experience to get everyone working together to bring it back up to a successful conclusion. Even when experienced energy workers are among the group, it can be hard to turn that pudding into a workable cone – this is mainly due to lack of co-ordination and coherence and can easily be avoided.

Nobody, with the exception, perhaps, of those very new to Wicca and its rituals, will get any real benefit from a pudding of power, although it is common but unspoken of for people to congratulate each other on a fantastic ritual even when it has actually been a bit of a flop. At any ritual gathering, the organisers should be prepared for the possibility of puddings and can take simple steps to avoid them.

> 1. Have designated people to 'keep' the circle as others raise the energy. These people will make sure the candles or fire are safe, that no-one looks as though they are about to pass out through exhaustion and they will take care of unexpected things like the ringing telephone you forgot to switch off.
>
> 2. Post 'sentries' at each of the quarters – their job is to encourage people around them to raise as much energy as they can. The sentries should also make sure that people are not getting too carried away and starting to 'space-out'.

3. Brief everyone beforehand, letting them know what to expect during the power raising and telling them of any pre-arranged signals they need to watch out for.

4. When drumming or music is used as an aide to ritual, have a signal at which this will be completely stopped, a few minutes before the energy starts to peak. If the drummers haven't got a queue to follow, they will not always stop immediately and participants can then be encouraged to carry on and the power is held back instead of being released, creating an anti-climax which brings the energy down to the pudding level again.

5. Have a definite signal given by an experienced Priestess or Priest, indicating to everyone that this is the point to release the power. When people see this signal, the Priest/ess can then lead the rest of the group in first releasing the energy and then slowly lowering to the floor to ground any excess energy and reconnect to the earth.

Hopefully these few easy steps will ensure that any group can raise a cone of power successfully and leave the pudding where it is supposed to be – on the table for a celebratory feast after the sacred space has been opened.

Sex Magic

Witchcraft is mistakenly associated with ritual sex and although this is something which happens from time to time, it not done as a matter of course but as a way of raising powerful energy for clearly defined purposes.

There is no place in Wicca for people who want to have an orgy or partake in voyeurism of any kind and no-one should be coerced into having sex for any reason, including initiation, no matter what anyone tells you. Sex magic should only ever take place between a couple who are already established lovers, in private and only for positive magical purposes. The high levels of energy involved in sex-magic could lead to power attractions, uncomfortable relationships in future workings, not to mention the risk of spreading disease or unwanted pregnancy if necessary physical precautions are not taken care of.

Sex magic is the balancing of polarities and bringing the masculine and feminine forces together in this way for magic is almost guaranteed to ensure positive results for all concerned. It is the union of the Goddess and God manifested physically and should be treated with respect and courtesy. If the couple are part of a larger group the other members do not need to know the details of what happened and the couple are under no obligation to tell them, although they are free to say anything that may be useful, for example, if they gained some vision or insight from the experience which relates directly to the spell they were working.

Having prepared for the ritual and cast a circle, everyone present will leave the couple alone in the room until they are called back in. The couple will keep the aim of the spell in mind throughout their love-making and clearly focus on the result being achieved, perhaps vocalising and whispering the desire to one another, building up the energy as they reach climax, at which point they will both visualise it being released and coming true. There could hardly be a better time for positive visualisation of results than the cosy aftermath of joyful love-making with your partner.

6

The Sacred Journey

Witches may not be able to fly in this world without the use of an airplane, but we can journey into the hidden realities of the Upperworld and Underworld and anything is possible in these realms, such as a trip to the stars on the back of a flying dragon. As we travel through these journey lands we can call upon our guardian spirits and animal guides, speak with the Goddess and God, meet with mythical archetypes, speak to our ancestors and question our inner self, the deep subconscious and the collective unconscious levels of the human psyche.

Journey, trance, walking between the worlds; it is called different things in different cultures. Perhaps associated more with Shamanism than Wicca, the tradition of taking inner journeys goes a long way back through history and has been practiced in almost every corner of the globe for centuries by our ancestors. It is an altered state of consciousness that allows the shaman or witch to receive intuition, advice and guidance. The shaman who practiced these techniques (and in many places still does) usually had a pharmacopoeia of hallucinogenic plants to achieve and enhance the journey state and tribal elders would call upon the shaman to journey for answers to problems affecting the whole community. Wicca does not advocate the taking of any such hallucinogenic preparations as we have different techniques we can use to journey.

Journey is not the same as guided meditation or visualisation – in those processes you have a speaker telling you where to go, what to do and what to look out for. Guided visualisation can certainly be useful but Journey is different – what happens is more spontaneous and free, the trance state is deeper and there are only guidelines, rather than rigid instructions, to guide you through the experience.

Journey takes place on a deep, subconscious level and the experiences one has in journey are very real indeed; just as every person and item has an astral double, so the journey, the astral experience, also has its physical counterparts. There are many cases where situations encountered in journey have been played out in ordinary life a few days or weeks later.

A journey can last for around fifteen minutes to begin with and up to an hour and a half or even longer as you gain experience, depending on the depth of the trance-state and the reasons for your journey. Time warps in strange ways when journeying and what is only half an hour in reality might seem like hours or just a few minutes in journey. Don't be taken by surprise if you find that an hour has passed when you had intended to come back in twenty minutes.

Although the journey is taken with little or no instruction, the ideal situation is to have at least one live drummer present (although drumming tapes can be bought inexpensively for this purpose if drummers are not available) providing a steady, fast beat throughout the journey and a rapid, broken and hard drumming towards the end of the allotted time to provide a call-back signal, alerting the journeyer that it is time to finish the journey and return to normality. Journey can be also done without a drum and is no less effective or sacred either way. Try listening to the drums and see if it suits you. Some people find drumming distracting, others find it helps them drift into an altered state of consciousness.

The first journey the novice undertakes should be done with the intention of finding a Place of Power. This will be the starting point for every future journey and provides a safe space to return to in journeys where you are uncomfortable or feel threatened. The place of power can be somewhere you actually know or somewhere you would like to be; the seaside, a cave, the middle of a forest or the summit of mountain. It is different for every person, the only common aspect being that you feel safe and nurtured in this place. The place of power is where you meet your guide and begin journeys to the upper and lower worlds.

The next journey, which may be done during the same session as finding your place of power, will be to meet with a totem animal or guardian who will serve as a guide through your journeys and can take you to meet other creatures and beings who inhabit the Upper and Under worlds. Your guide will show you where you can meet with elementals and the Goddess and God, as well as other archetypes and will be able to answer any questions you have or tell you how and where to get the answers.

The inner guide might be a totem animal or a person. Whether your guide is animal or human, you can ask them what you need to know and why they have come to you, what wisdom do they have to pass on to you? Animal or human, talk to the guide and build up a relationship with them and they will serve you well in the hidden realms. It is common for people to have different guides for the upper and under worlds, some people have many guides at different times; whatever the case, they will offer assistance and advice in whatever way they can. Occasionally a guide will leave you, sometimes giving reasons, sometimes not; in these cases, you can call for another guide to take its place.

Preparing for Journey
Cleanse your aura and the space you are working in and open your chakras. Cast your circle as you normally would, paying particular attention on requesting the elementals to protect you as you journey. Turn off the telephone and make sure you will be warm and comfortable for the next hour or so.

To enter the trance state we need for journey, it is essential to be relaxed fully, so that the mind is able to drift off to the altered state of consciousness in which journey takes place. Once the relaxed state of mind is achieved, the journey can begin with finding your place of power. The rainbow countdown described here is only one of many ways to reach the journey-state. Many witches find they can enter the right state of mind almost at will, with practice and experience.

The Rainbow Countdown
Lie down or sit in a comfortable chair, do not fold your arms or cross your legs. Take a few minutes to relax yourself with a few deep breaths or by clenching and relaxing all the muscles in your body in turn. Another way of achieving a deeply relaxed state is to imagine you are being bathed in a warm light which flows gently from the top of your head down your body, soothing away tension or anxiety as it creeps downwards. Repeat the process until you feel very comfortable.

Imagine you are surrounded by red light, you are suspended in red sea, imagine there is red everywhere, try to see it clearly. Let the red wash all over you and gradually it becomes…

Orange, you are bathed in an orange glow. Let yourself be carried on waves of orange, orange sea, orange sky, the orange is all around you and then it changes to…

Yellow light is around you, you are relaxing deeper into the yellow light and yellow waves wash over you, you are surrounded by yellow and it becomes.

Green light supports you, green is all around, feel how lovely the green is, soothing green relaxes you further, green becomes…

Blue light, you are surrounded by blue. It soothes you, taking you further away from normality and the blue becomes…

Purple and the purple sends you even further into a relaxed state and at last changes to a brilliant bright…

White light and the white light is everywhere. The white light becomes misty and when it clears you find yourself in…

The Place of Power

As the mists of white light begin to clear, imagine you are standing in some natural place, see it all around you. How does it feel here? Are you happy? Are there plants, animals? Is it day or night? Noisy or quiet? Take a look around, explore every inch of it and assess how comfortable and safe you feel here. If it doesn't quite feel right, then ask for the mists to return and then clear again to reveal another place that will be more suitable.

Follow your intuition and when you find a place that feels right for you, take time to become acquainted with it. Feel the power of the earth surging beneath you, the water in a nearby stream, the warmth of the sun all around you, feel the fresh air against your skin. Feel the connection you have with all life and draw your finger clockwise around your space to cast a magic circle. You don't need candles or incense here as the elements are all around you and you are already in a circle. You are in your place of power. Say so in whatever words come to you. Ask the elements and the place itself to always be here for you, to be a place of power and protection for you and you alone. State that this is your sacred space.

From here, you can take long walks, set sail on the ocean, climb crags and fly with the eagles. Anywhere you want to visit can be reached from here and you may return at any time and draw energy from this place of power whenever you have need of it.

Coming Back

When you decide your journey is finished, wherever you are in the upper or lower worlds, you should always return to your place of power. If you are working with a drummer or drumming tape which gives a call-back signal, this indicates that the session will stop soon and provides you with adequate time to come back to the place of power and go through the 'waking up' procedure. Travel back to it through all the same routes that you took on the way to other places in the realm. Give thanks to the elements and the guardians of the place for their protection.

Visualise a mist forming in your place of power, a white mist that enfolds gently around you. Follow the rainbow countdown in reverse, feel yourself lifting slightly out of your relaxed state, in a moment the white light becomes...

Purple and the purple surrounds and supports you and changes to...

Blue and in the blue you begin to feel yourself breathing, not faster or slower or deeper, just normal but you feel it and the blue becomes...

Green and the green light makes you aware of the sounds in the room you lie in and then...

Yellow light is all around you and the yellow begins to make you feel your body and now...

Orange light is everywhere, a gentle orange glow - wriggle your toes and imagine...

Red light supporting you and the red begins to clear and you can move your body...

Gently begin to wake up and open your eyes when you are ready to be back in 'reality'.

Take plenty of time afterwards to gather yourself up, have a stretch or shake your hands and feet. Make notes on your journey to assess your progress and refer back to your notes over the next few days to see if there is any connection between the journey and your daily life.

Common practice after journeys and rituals of any kind among the vast majority of Wiccans is to have something to eat and drink as a way of grounding. After this, the elements and Goddess and God should be thanked as normal and the circle opened. Remember to keep any promise of offerings that you made.

The Inner Guide

Once you have found your place of power, you are ready to meet with a guardian or totem animal who can show around the hidden worlds. The next journey could be done as part of the same journey in which you found your place of power or you might want to close up the journey session and continue with this exercise another time. Go with whatever feels right for you, there is no right or wrong. This journey, and indeed all journeys you undertake, should be done within a fully cast magic circle in the physical reality.

Go through the same procedure as before to reach your place of power, you will find with practice that the journey state becomes easier to reach.

Start in your place of power and state clearly your intentions to find a guide. Ask for a pathway to lead you to a place where you can meet your guide.

As you see a path appear, start walking, it might be a woodland path, through a mountain pass or open fields or beach.

The path will lead you to a place where your guide will appear. Stand tall and proud and ask in your own words that a Guide comes to you. For example:

> *I*, (Name), *ask that my inner guide comes to me now in this place with perfect love and perfect trust.*

Now see who comes to you. Man or Woman? Worm or Stag? Eagle or Wood Pigeon?

Greet your guardian and smile, introduce yourself and see what they have to say to you. Use your intuition to judge if this guide is worthy of you and ask any questions you may have about them. You need to know that this is the right guide for you and they will not mind this inquisitiveness.

There are no right or wrong ways to begin building up a relationship with your guide, but polite manners would be a good way to start. Find out their name and give them yours, exchange information, say why you are here and what you hope to gain from the experience.

When you feel that you have gained enough from this initial meeting, ask if you can call on them again and if there is any gift you can bring with you next time as a token of trust and friendship.

Follow the procedure for coming out of journey and when you feel ready, come back to the here and now. Having something to eat and drink will help to settle you back in the present moment.

After you find your guide you can do some research into what your guide, if it is an animal, represents. This will help you to understand why that particular animal has chosen to be your guide, giving you insights as to what qualities you need to develop or get rid of in your life.

Each animal has mystical and physical qualities associated with it and these qualities may be related to current or ongoing events in our lives and can provide information or guidelines for us to follow. For example, if you have a fear of an animal, like spiders, then a spider might appear to you as an indication that you need to face the fears in your life head on and move past them. A butterfly might indicate that you need to stop placing restrictions on yourself and be free to move into new areas of life, to be more light-hearted and carefree.

Good descriptions of animal qualities, both physical and mystical, can be found in many books, especially those dealing with the subject of Shamanism. Information on the natural, physical qualities of a particular animal will also prove useful. You can, of course, simply ask your guide why it has come to you and what qualities or inspirations can be gained through meeting and talking with each other. Guides are here to help us find out more about ourselves, our subconscious levels of understanding, our deepest buried emotions and fears or hopes. Asking your guide about issues that concern you and talking over things in the journey state is a good way of getting to know yourself better and continue your spiritual development.

A guide also works as a navigator, showing you the secret pathways and routes through the mystery realms. You can ask your guide to take you on a tour of the realms and show you things of particular interest or value.

As mentioned earlier, there may be times when a guide leaves you and is replaced by another. This can be due to several reasons. Perhaps your guide is on a spiritual path of its own and serving as your guide is part of its development that has now been completed; the guide can then continue on its own path. Another reason is that the guide is assigned to you to show you something specific that ties in with its properties. This guide will disappear when you have followed its advice and moved past any blockage or obstacles in your life that the animal symbolised.

If your guide tells you it needs to leave you, give thanks to them for the time they have spent with you and for their advice and guidance through the journey worlds. Then follow the process of seeking out a new guide and greet this one with enthusiasm, for he or she will be just as valuable to you as the last guide.

Journeying Onwards

Journey can give us answers and set our minds at ease and we can often find comfort in talking with the guides and creatures we meet in the other worlds. If you want answers to a particular question you can go into a journey and ask your guide to take you to someone who can help with that specific issue or perhaps your guide will be able to help you.

As well as helping us to deal with our own situations and problems, we can undergo journeys to find out how we can best help others. For example, ask your guide to take you to a wise woman or shamanic healer for advice on which method of healing or magic would suit a particular person.

Another good reason for you to journey is to meet with your Anima or Animus and integrate the qualities of your opposite gender into your life, providing you with balance and harmony. It also gives you opportunity to explore these aspects of yourself and integrate them into your life if you choose. The Anima is the hidden feminine quality in men and the Animus is the hidden masculine element of women.

Journey can also be done with the intention of connecting to the Goddess and God and each of the elements. Whatever your reasons for journey, you should remember to cast a circle in the physical plane first.

As with other aspects of Wicca there are different teachings from across the globe about how the realms outside our normal consciousness are defined and perceived. One of the most commonly used in Wicca is the idea of upper and lower worlds, with the real, physical world being between the two, like a tree spreading roots below (the lower world) and branches (the upper world) above the trunk (the physical world). In these places we can have different types of journey.

Normally the upper world is associated with intellect, the thinking processes and it is here that we can learn how to develop our spirituality and gain insight and intuition. The lower, or under, world is a more shadowy place where our Anima or Animus can be found. The lower world is where we can uncover aspects of our psyche that we have hidden, deliberately or otherwise, and begin to work with them to restore balance in our consciousness.

Journeys are always done with some intention in mind but are very often surprising in the way they turn out when you set out with specific goals. If you have a question you want answers to, your guide will take you to the most appropriate personality to give you answers but don't be surprised if that turns out to be an insect telling you to put out your antennae and find out for yourself.

Throughout this book, further journeys are suggested but there is no need to do any of them if you do not feel the need to explore journey further. Drumming can be done with any of the further journeys but is not a requirement, only a preference, as with everything else in Wicca, you will find out through experience the best ways of doing things yourself.

7

The God and Goddess

Wicca has a God and a Goddess. Or, rather, we have many Gods. There are myriad Goddesses and Gods across the world and in the eclectic religion of Wicca, we can use any and all whom we find appropriate to our rites or to whom we are drawn on a personal level. While it may seem on the surface that Wicca does strive to be a balanced faith, acknowledging the God and Goddess, it is unfortunate that too many groups or individuals are actually paying greater homage to women and the Goddess. Although men will usually identify more strongly with the God and women with the Goddess because of our natural gender, to fully integrate both masculine and feminine aspects of deity within Wicca is essential in bringing balance to our lives and our magic.

Although most witches think of them as Goddess and God, this is only a way of relating to the much bigger Universal All. Naming the qualities of the All as Goddess or God gives us a vision or image that is easier to relate to than some nameless force we cannot see, touch or hear in the ordinary ways.

There isn't one word for the divine that works well for everybody. Some say Great Spirit, others refer to the All, the Mysterious Ones, or the Old Ones. Whatever we choose to call our personal vision of deity, there are many aspects to it, yet it all comes from the same source – the universal energy and spirit that binds everything together.

The Goddess and God are not seen as physical beings, watching over us from above to control or punish us. Rather, they are the embodiment of our connections with everything else, our Great Mother and Father figures are there to give us strength and guidance. The different Goddess and God aspects can be drawn down into our magic circle and when we ask for their help or blessing or strength or healing, we are appealing to the universe to bend to our will and bring us what we need.

Each of the Goddesses and Gods have different aspects we can draw on, so whatever the occasion, there will be at least one or two who can be called upon to lend their influence. It would be wise to check that the Goddess and God you work with for a ritual do not have conflicting interests or agendas before bringing them together in your circle, however.

When working in a group, the Goddess and God are often referred to as Lord and Lady or the Old Ones as each witch has their personal favourites and this makes invoking simpler. Some of the most commonly used names are listed below with their attributes

The Wiccan Goddess

Worshipped in every culture world-wide, the Goddess is normally seen as a benevolent mother with pregnant belly and full breasts. She has a light side and a dark side, for she is woman in all her aspects – innocent and pure, a healer, a lover, a nurturing mother and also the one who tends the dying and sees their passage to the underworld.

Aradia - Aradia is the daughter of the Goddess Diana, Queen of the Witches. Diana, disguised as a mortal woman, came to teach witchcraft and mysteries to humans. She eventually had to reveal herself as a Goddess and so sent her daughter, Aradia, to earth in her place. Aradia was particularly concerned with defeating oppression of earth's peoples and used magic to do this. She can be called down to help us when we face adversity, persecution and oppression.

Artemis – Greek Goddess of the new moon, twinned with Apollo, she rules psychic work, healing and protection. Sometimes associated with animals, especially bears and also with the star constellation Ursa Major. Artemis is often depicted with a bow and arrow in her protective aspect. Her roman name is Diana.

Brigid / Bride – the Goddess of Fire, ruling Mars and the Moon. She is the triple Goddess of poetry, healing and smith craft, a Warrior Goddess, protector and preserver. She is strong and wise. Call on her to help protect your children in a tough situation. As Bride she is revered at the Sabbat of Imbolc.

Cerridwen - Goddess of the Cauldron of life. Moon Goddess. Psychic work, healing and protection. Her cauldron is the source of life and inspiration, knowledge and beauty. We can journey to drink from her cauldron to gain wisdom and intuitions.

Dana – the welsh Goddess of the ancient faerie tradition, she is the mother of the earth and her people were the Tuatha De Danaan, the lost people of ancient Britain.

Diana – the moon Goddess and hunter, she is often depicted with a dog or hare at her side and also with a bow and arrow. Diana is an ancient Roman Goddess, equivalent to the Greek Artemis. She was chief hunter to the gods also the goddess of nature, and of the harvest. She is guardian of springs and streams and the protector of wild animals. A strong figure who can protect us and teach us. Diana was said to appear to mortal women to teach the mysteries of witchcraft until she sent her daughter Aradia to take her place.

Epona - Protector and patron of horses, Epona is closely linked to the Uffington White Horse chalk figure, which some believe was made to honour her. She is the only Celtic Goddess to have been worshipped in Rome. She is associated with fertility and it is said that couples who are trying to conceive a child cannot fail in this if they visit the white horse at Uffington and perform their special magic upon it! Epona has also been known as the Great Mother Goddess and Rhiannon in Wales.

Freya – (also Frigg or Freyja) the Norse Goddess of sex, fertility, war and wealth. She was wife/sister to Odin and Friday was named for her. Her planet is Venus and she gives us love and courage.

Gaia – Mother Earth. Of all the Goddesses, she is the most ancient and widely worshipped of all. Statues and carvings of her are found world-wide. She has many other names, but the modern version tends to be Gaia. She is heavily pregnant and has full, pendulous breasts. She is the embodiment of earth's consciousness and very much the mother of us all. She wants to look after her children and gives us security, health and material possessions. She nurtures us, as any mother would love and nurture her children. Speak to Gaia for comfort in times of need and invoke her presence when working magically to heal the earth and for energy and help for environmental actions, especially when invoked in conjunction with Pan.

Hecate – Greek Goddess of the Underworld and the Dark Moon, often seen as a triple Goddess. Her planet is Saturn, and she can have quite dark leanings. Ask for her help with psychic matters, divinations, healing and protection. She brings inspiration and creativity to those who honour her but she has no time for those who do her wrong. She is a great protector of women and especially witches.

Kali – The Hindu Goddess of both birth and destruction. She condemns all violence against women and ancient witches would call her up to help with their hexes. As a giver of birth, however, she is also has powerful creative energies we can call upon.

Moirae - the three fates, who spin, weave and cut the threads of mortal life and fate. Clotho spins the thread to start a life, Lachesis measures the thread with chance and Atropos is the one who cuts the thread to end a life. The Norse fates are called the Norns.

Morrigan - Celtic goddess of war and death who hovered over the battlefield as a crow or raven.

Selene – Goddess of the moon, and protector of witches, Selene is benevolent and giving. Also as Moon Goddess, She presides over women's mysteries and psychic powers. Seek Her when you feel confused and need to bring Her light and clarity to bear upon a problem.

Triple Goddess of the Moon – Virgin, Mother, Crone - the moon and the Goddess are closely linked and most Goddesses are related to the moon in some way. The three moon phases tie in with the Goddess in this way – new and waxing moon are the Virgin Goddess, young, innocent, perhaps even naïve, the lover and temptress – full moon is the Mother Goddess, pregnant with a horde of children, she protects and nurtures, giving of herself for others – waning and dark moon are the Crone Goddess – the old hag who has seen it all, done it all; wise, knowledgeable; the healer and midwife but also the reaper of souls, she is the Goddess of the death and the underworld.

The Wiccan God

The Wiccan God also has many guises and, like the Goddess, he can be found throughout history and across the world. He is best known to Wiccans as the Green Man or Pan of the woods. The God is Consort to the Goddess and rules beside her, not over her. The God represents men in all their aspects - young and bold, strong and protective, wise and forceful. He is also sensitive and laughing, loving and playful.

Apollo - Greek God, brother to the Goddess Artemis. He is a God of the sun and light, medicine and intellect, poetry and music.

Bran - the Welsh giant of prophecy, the arts, war, music and writing. Many legends of Bran's adventures tell of his strength, health and self-sacrifice for the good of his people. Bran watches over all those who call upon him. He will fight for you and sacrifice himself for your benefit. It is particularly helpful to invoke him if you are feeling weak in body and/or spirit and require the fortification Bran can bestow

Cernunnos - The Celtic Horned God associated with fertility and wealth, especially associated with several horned animals but especially the stag. He is the God of Nature and loves deep, dark forests. Cernunnos is associated with the Cerne Abbas chalk figure (with its obvious fertility symbol) and is said to lead the wild hunt across the sky in times of national crisis.

The Green Man - The male spirit of nature, life and growth. He is the male counterpart of Gaia. Green Man carvings are found all over in Christian churches, often seen sticking out his tongue - in protest at being penned up inside where he cannot hear the call of the wild or in protest of Christianity, who knows?

Herne The Hunter – Another Horned God, Herne is another aspect of Cernunnos. He has antlers and is closely associated with the stag he hunts. The dark lord, God of the hunt, wild animals, and forests. He is the hunter and the hunted, protected and protector. Call on Herne for strength and determination.

Lugh - An Irish God of craftsmanship and skilled work. As a solar deity he is celebrated at the festival of Lughnasadh, literally meaning festival of Lugh. This celebrates the first corn of the harvest.

Odin – God of war, magic and cunning. It is from Odin that we get the divinatory rune stones. His familiars are the Raven and the Wolf, his wife was Freya. He is depicted as a fearsome God and in his old age was a God of Wisdom and psychic sight. Odin can bestow you with strength, heroism and triumph.

Pan – the Greek God of Nature, he is wild, horned and horny. The rutting, goat-footed God who lives with luscious, wild abandon in green woodlands. He is the God of music, fertility, and dance. Pan can also be invoked and called upon to aid in magical protection during protests or actions to do with earth conservation and as he is from the same pantheon as Gaia, the two would work well together in rituals for earth healing and protection.

Thoth - The Egyptian ibis-headed God of wisdom, the moon, science, literature and magic. Thoth is connected with magical writings and the tarot. He is said to have been the first magician and is the patron God of ritual magic.

The Cycle of the Goddess and God

The Sun God and Moon Goddess have their individual cycles that repeat themselves throughout the year and within these cycles they also interact with one another. The Wiccan year is based around eight festivals, the Sabbats, and the story of the Goddess and God coincides with these festivals.

The Moon Goddess is triple, maiden, mother and crone and although there are thirteen lunar cycles each year, the Goddess also has a single cycle which lasts through one full year.

The Sun God has two aspects, Oak King and Holly King, waxing and waning, and this cycle is seen every day as the sun rises and sets, but also lasts for one full year.

At the beginning of the year, both Goddess and God are young, having been reborn at the winter solstice festival of Yule. The Goddess is Bride at Imbolc and corn from the previous year's harvest is made into a corn dolly to represent her. Wiccans often make a 'Bridie bed' for the corn dolly and invite her to bring a good harvest as the first seeds are sown in the earth. She is virginal and in her maiden phase as the new year waxes. The Sun God is young and brash, beginning to strengthen as the days begin to grow longer.

As the days grow longer, towards the festival of Beltane, the Goddess becomes playful, she is still in her maiden aspect and starts to tease the God. He is not deterred and chases her, finally they mate and the Goddess begins to change from Maiden to Mother, the God gaining further strength with the warmth of summer. He is the Lord of the woodlands, the strong protector and father figure. As the strong and virile Oak King, he knows his rule of the sun is soon to end as he dances and hunts in the forest.

The summer solstice brings a change for the God, from Oak King to Holly King. They fight each other and the Holly King stands victorious. The Goddess is beginning to swell with pregnancy in her Mother phase, she stands over nature, lending her energy to nurture all growing and living things. The earth is abundant, warm and generous with gifts.

At harvest time, the Goddess and God give their gifts to us, the God now seen as a wise man, a shaman and healer. He starts to draw the nights in and becomes consort to the Goddess as she lets go of her children and begins to age.

When the Goddess becomes the Crone towards the year's end around the time of Samhain, she is seen as wise and intelligent, yet with a dark side – she is an old woman who knows of death and decay and for these reasons she is often feared. The Holly King represents darkness and death with the waning of the sun in the depth of winter. The earth is bare, cold and dark. But without death and decay there could be no life, no joy. It is only through knowing hardship and loss that we can appreciate beauty and innocence.

At the mid-winter solstice, it is time for the Oak King to slay his brother, the Holly King and as he does so, the Crone Goddess resigns her place and gives birth to the new Maiden Goddess and the cycle continues. The sun will begin to warm the world again and the Goddess and God will continue to give us their strength and love.

Journey to meet with the Goddess and God

A sacred journey to meet the Goddess and God should not be undertaken lightly and it is worth taking time to meditate on your purposes for this journey for at least a week or preferably longer beforehand.

During this time, try to find out more about the particular aspect of deity you want to meet. If there is a Goddess or God you feel drawn to, visit places which are relevant to them, seek out paintings, poetry and knowledge of the deity and look more closely into the myths and legends surrounding them.

Think about your reasons for going into the journey. How would connecting to this specific deity help you in your daily life? Are you looking for advice as you advance along the Wiccan path? Do you have life changing decisions to make that you need help with? Do you want to bring the qualities of this Goddess or God into your life? If there is no particular Goddess you want to meet, ask for the Triple Goddess to come to you.

Cast a circle as you have done before and go into the journey state by deep relaxation and visit your place of power.

Start your journey by asking your guide to appear and lead you to a safe place where you can meet with the Goddess. On the path to meet the Goddess, notice what kind of land you are passing through; is it dark or light? Are there any obstacles in your way or people and animals to meet along the way?

When you come to the designated place, ask your guide to come back when it is time to leave and guide you back to your place of power.

Be still and silent, breathe a few deep breaths. Ask for the Goddess to come to you. As she greets you, be respectful, but remember that she is loving and kind, full of humour and compassion. She is a triple Goddess and you can ask to meet each aspect of her in turn or ask her to come to you in whatever guise is most relevant for your life at this moment.

Once you are done, or, if journeying to a drum, when you hear the call back, give thanks and ask any final questions. At this point, if your guide is not present, ask them to return and lead you back. Follow your guide along the path back to your place of power, noticing if the land has changed, if obstacles have been removed or if you can see and hear anything that seems significant in light of your conversation with the Goddess.

Come back to the present moment by breathing yourself through the chakra/rainbow colours and write down a record of your journey. Carry out the usual precautions of grounding or eating after closing your circle.

Wait at least a month before following the journey process again to meet the God; this gives you time to reflect and meditate on your experience and find out more about the Goddess to verify what happened during journey. Again, make notes of your experience and anything you were told during the journey as these snippets of wisdom, however vague or seemingly irrelevant, can sometimes prove useful at a later date.

8

The Elements of Wicca

In order to bring peace, healing and harmony to our lives and those of our friends and neighbours through the art of spell casting, we must have some knowledge of how the elements invoked during our circle casting provide necessary contributions to our magic.

We invoke these elements so that the essence, or core energy, of each is present for the whole of the ritual, thereby adding the element's specific qualities to any magical work we are doing.

Earth represents the practical and material aspects of the ritual, providing focus and a base to work from. Air represents our thoughts, the communication and mental focus required. Fire is our passion and courage, giving us the desire and energy required to reach a positive outcome. Water balances our emotions and supports us, we use water to change the tides that flow against our wishes. Spirit is the binding element that holds all the others together and the driving force, the will power and intention we ourselves bring to the magic.

All the elaborate ritual texts or beautiful poetry in the world will not invoke the elements unless we know what each element represents. In order to gain this understanding, each element is discussed here with examples of how to cast a

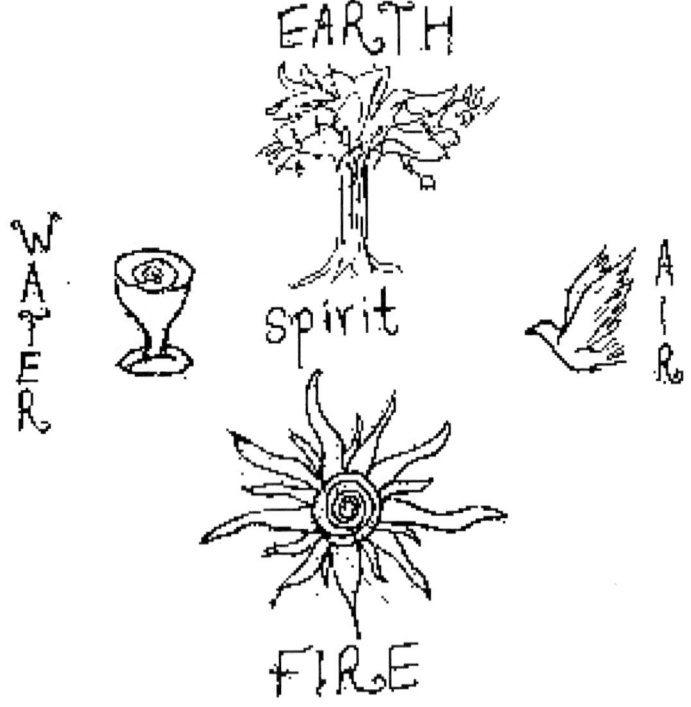

circle using the element and simple ideas for element based spells.

Earth

Earth is our material world. It is the physical things that make up our bodies, our homes, our gardens. Our food grows in the earth, we sit and walk and lie on it, we can make fire from earth to warm us. The earth supports our bodies all the time. It shelters us with caves or brick houses or a broad-leaved tree. All creatures are part of the earth. So are plants and rocks, mountains, hair, paper and flowers.

Earth is about fertility, pregnancy, nurturing love, children, harvesting, planting, material possessions, decay, compost, ornaments, clay, forests. We eat food that grows in the earth, we wear the skins (leather) of earth's animals. We entrust the bodies of our beloved dead to the care of the earth.

Everywhere you look, earth is around you. Go out into nature, stare out of the office window or look inside your house and make a list of everything you see that has come, in one shape or another, from the earth. You will have a long list and this is only the beginning. Once you see how much earth you have in your life, you start to appreciate it more.

When we enter a cave we go into the belly of the earth, we are surrounded by rock and darkness and eerie silence, we can sit and meditate and go on sacred journeys to the underworld, in caves we can do powerful rejuvenating magic and emerge reborn. Caves connect us to the primal power of the Old Ones and where else could we be more 'grounded' than in a deep dark womb-like cave?

Trees, forests and woodland can whisper to us on the breeze, ground us with their roots, provide shelter, food and ornamentation. Each tree has a different meaning, for me oak is very special. We can stand tall with our backs to a tree, hug a tree, tell it our fears and secret desires, they can answer us with intuitive flashes of understanding. Trees have guardians and they can talk to us to, we just need to take time and be still, quiet and patient to hear their voices. Trees give us gifts too, and if they like us enough they will point out something particular for us and us alone.

Long-barrows and cairns, standing stones, ancient mountains and the rocky crevasses are also places of great earthiness. The ancient sites of our heritage can give us transforming insights to the nature of problems, can be the starting point of underworld journeys and provide refreshment and revitalise us.

Magical Associations

Earth is said to be in the North quarter of the circle and the altar is placed in the North with a representation of earth upon it, such as a crystal, dish of earth, wooden statue.

The primary earth Goddess is Mother Nature, Gaia.

Earth represents the dark of winter at midnight.

The astrological signs of earth are Taurus, Virgo and Capricorn.

All life comes from the earth and we are all deeply connected to and rooted in the earth. We are part of it, not some separate organism designed to exploit or dominate the earth.

Earth is used in our rituals to bring us stability and security. It represents the manifestation of desire and completion.

The tools of earth are crystals, the pentacle, stone, wooden wands, soil, food, flowers, fabric and metal, herbs and jewellery.

The elemental spirits of earth are tree-spirits, dryads and gnomes, mythical earth beings are, among others, trolls and fairies.

Earth colours are brown, black, green and gold.

Earth spells are done for fertility, growth, maturing and nurturing, family matters, healing, material issues, practical matters, stability, completion and fulfilment, bringing things to fruition.

Working with Earth

To cleanse yourself and your sacred space using earth, gather some sweet smelling herbs or flowers to place in the room. Take a few twigs or leaves and tie them into a bundle and use these to dust off your aura, asking for unwanted energy to return to the earth.

Although the circle is normally cast by visualising and directing a barrier of energy to create a circle around us, we can also use an element to cast the circle.

Find something earthy and pointed to use to as an extension of your aura, a wooden wand, a twig, crystal or even a bone. Prepare your sacred space by clearing away the clutter and go through a cleansing exercise and open your chakras.

Take your pointy piece of earth and think about the barriers we can create with earth; a mud-built hut, a wall of trees, a spinning shield of leaves or a cobbled surface. Walk the circle perimeter, focusing on creating an earth barrier, an energy circle made entirely of earth. Feel energy flowing through your body, down your arm and out through the earth extension of yourself to create the circle.

Invoke each element and when you come to earth, bring all those powerful images and all your knowledge of earth to mind as you speak. Feel the earth as your body, the earth under your feet. Holding a ritual out of doors provides an opportunity to touch the earth itself as you call out your invocation.

Ask for the presence of the Goddess as Gaia and the God as the Green Man or Herne the Hunter, ask for the female and male qualities of earth to be present in your circle and bear in mind that you are also a representative of earth and a daughter or son of the earth.

If you are outside, feel your feet on the ground and wiggle your toes, reach down to touch the earth with your fingers and dig around with your forefinger until it is dirty. Mark your forehead, the third eye chakra, with this physical symbol of the earth as your connection to it.

Sit in your circle and spend some time meditating on what you have found out about earth, both through research and from your personal experience. Think about what earth does for you, physically and spiritually, how you behave towards the earth and the attitudes you have about it. No teacher can tell you what earth is, it is something you know within yourself and you can uncover that now. Make notes on anything that comes to you as you sit with earth, perhaps holding a piece of it in your hands, smoothing it, as you spend this time reflecting.

Think of someone or something you want to help and use the examples given below to create an earth spell suitable for your purpose. The best spells are those we create intuitively as we are more able to relate to our own ideas as opposed to those which have been pre-formulated by someone we have never met who has no knowledge of the circumstances surrounding our need for the magic.

Once you have cast your spell, by consecrating a crystal to offer to your friend for example, you need to raise a cone of power to energise the spell and release that energy into the universe, along the web of life, to bring the results to you.

You can raise a cone of power using earth in many ways, rattle, drum, dance, shake your body, clap your hands. All of these actions use the earth of your body, your primary Wiccan tool. Think of a chant or a single word that is relevant to what you hope to achieve, healing, pregnancy, wealth, happiness. As you raise the energy, feel it build up into a cone shape and release it with a big whoosh.

Ground yourself straight away by shaking your hands and stamping your feet or touching your forehead to the ground. Stay this way for as long as necessary for you to feel grounded and solid again.

Consecrate some earthy food and drink with the element of earth, asking Gaia and the Green Man to bless your ritual. Something like baked potatoes or granary bread and apple juice or cider would be appropriate, taste these gifts of the earth and be thankful for earth in your life.

Give thanks to the Goddess and God and thanks to earth, close your circle in reverse order to the way you cast it. If you still feel spaced out or heady, tidying up your circle and packing away any ritual equipment should help.

Earth Spells

Earth Grows: You could write a wish for something new in your life and bury the paper with a seed on top, water it in and let it grow, focusing thoughts and directing energy to it each time you see the seed poking out through the soil.

Earth Holds: To keep a secret you've been trusted with but are absolutely dying to tell someone about - tie a loose piece of cotton or silk (natural fibres) to a tree, telling the tree your secret and asking it to be a guardian of the secret and then keep your lips sealed and give the tree a gift, water on a hot day, tree food, tidy up the litter.

Earth Decays: To get rid of something that is no longer useful in your life, be it a situation or emotion, take an earth thing like a green leaf, a bit of natural wood or a slice of wholemeal bread and with focus and direction, throw it on a compost heap to decompose, asking that your unwanted issue be taken with it and so decay, gradually returning to the earth it came from and out of your life forever. Transforming and getting rid of things in this way can be a very healing experience if we put all our energy into it, but we must always bear in mind that it is never done with the intention of harming or getting rid of anyone. We only wish to get rid of our own emotions, hurt, grief or anger relating to people and any stress we have been caused by others.

Earth is Ordinary: Use your imagination and the everyday objects around you as inspiration for making earthy spells, plait flowers or herbs and ribbons together to keep under your pillow for dreams of solutions to your problems or make bread so you can pummel the dough to vent your anger.

Earth is Organic: Gardening can be a very useful Wiccan tool with an even more useful practical outcome. We can do gardening to plant seeds that represent our wishes and grow those seeds into food that we can use to adorn our altar at harvest time and later serve in delicious meals to our friends as a way of building community and companionship. Gardening is also the best way to ground yourself. Gardening can be used to get rid of anger by digging and weeding. Gardening connects us to nature in ways we can only experience for ourselves.

Earth is Solid: Wool, cotton, silk, hemp. All types of natural fabric can be used in our rituals. Cut out, sew and stuff a doll to represent a person you want to help and raise power over it to send to your friend as positive energy. For creative earth magic, think of something you want to bring into your life that relates to earth, the safe return of a straying cat for example. Find a few appropriate words and then start to weave or knit (a simple square will suffice) and with each twist of the wool say the words over and over again, as a mantra, imagining each time you say them, *kitty returns, safe kitty, kitty home.*

Earth Spirits

The best way to meet earth elementals is to go outside and speak to them. Spending time in the woods or open fields and walking through country parks will make you familiar with the natural energies of earth.

Find out where your local beauty spots are and start visiting them in turn, also go to earthy places that are not beautiful and serene but seem wild, overgrown and abandoned. Visit places which have little appeal to you as well as places you are drawn to. Nature is everywhere and the spirits of earth inhabit all places, the dark and gloomy as well as the sunlit and cheerful. It is only through getting to know our local earth centres that we can find somewhere that feels right for us to spend more time with on a regular basis.

If you feel called to somewhere with trees, then single out a tree that seems special. This might be a special tree or just one that you happen to walk past every day while walking the dog.

Having found a tree, visit it whenever you can. Go there in spring, summer, autumn and winter, in torrential rain, in snow and wind and dazzling sunshine. Take time to sit by the tree, bring it gifts of rich compost, water and speech. Talk to the tree and listen for answers. You can speak aloud, as the vibrations will resonate with the tree, or you could speak silently in your mind to the tree. You may 'hear' the tree talking back to you or you might see images or have the tree's thoughts drift into your mind and mix with your own thoughts. Whatever the case, if you are still, silent and respectful, the tree will appreciate your calm energy and your desire to communicate. Trees are connected to the earth by their roots and they move in the wind, they know about life and cycles. They are great givers of wisdom when we take the time to hear their words.

It may sound like folly to try and listen to the trees when there are other, more fun ways to spend a Sunday morning, if you persist, however, you will be rewarded. Their words are not heard by the ears, but by the mind or the heart. It may not be an immediate response, or even verbal one, the tree may speak to you by shedding a leaf in your path or by showing you visions or flashes of intuition. Be aware that there are many ways of perceiving, sound is just one and you might find that nature uses another medium of communication.

If you are not a tree person but prefer hill walking or caving, you could explore the spirit of earth within rocks or stones instead. Find a safe area to be where you can sit patiently and still to start the process of communication with a rock spirit. If you are drawn to a rock spirit, take time to sit with the rock and caress its surface, getting to know its shape, texture and feel. Rocks are great for providing sound advice and a faithful friend. A rock spirit, unlike the tree, has no moving parts or living roots, but rock can be shaped by wind, by water and covered with moss. Rock can provide shelter and comfort, they have a lot to teach us about stability, patience and the constant cycles of life.

As well as visiting earth elementals in the 'real' world, we can go on magical journeys to meet with the elementals of earth.

Carry out a cleansing exercise and open your chakras. Cast a circle and then lie down or sit comfortably and relax.

Start the journey in your place of power and ask for your guardian or guide to appear to you, welcome them, re-meet and establish contact just as you would an old friend.

Tell your guardian you would like to meet with an earth spirit and ask him/her to take you to meet one.

Follow your guide into the dark and winter land of earth, notice everything you see on the way; animals, plants, rocks. Your guide will lead you to the most appropriate place and leave you alone to communicate with earth spirits in private.

Ask an earth spirit to come to you and wait for it to appear. It may be a fairy or animal or perhaps more floral and leafy in appearance.

Greet the earth spirit and talk with it; ask questions, give answers, tell it why you are there and find out what you can do for the earth. Spend time walking with or sitting with or simply being with the earth spirit. Feel its nature, sense its power and dignity. Open each of your senses to what it shows you and when you feel you have been touched by the earth spirit in some way give your thanks and offer to do something special for the earth in return.

Ask for your guardian to lead you back to your place of power. Offer thanks and blessings and return slowly to the 'normal' world. Have something to eat and drink, leaving some as an offering to scatter on the earth.

Air

Without food we die slowly, without water we die within a few days. But without air it would take us only minutes to die. It is so vitally important to us and we use it in so many ways that we don't notice. Air is all around us, we breathe it, we see through it, sound is carried to us as vibrations in the air. Birds fly through the air, trees and flowers move in the air, leaves fall through it. Air is involved in so many things we do – the swing of a tennis racket, the throw of a ball, the breeze on our skin, aeroplanes and helicopters, parachute drops, even by simply walking we are moving through the element of air.

Take a deep breath right now. And another breath. Don't worry about how it tastes or smells or feels, just breathe and know that you are already communing with the element.

Air is in your lungs, trapped in the folds of your clothing and the hairs of your body. Air is perhaps the most important of the elements in some respects as it represents our thinking, intellectual processes and it is through air that we can communicate with others.

There is nowhere we can go to on earth that does not have an air supply. The air at the top of the highest mountain will be different to the air at sea-level in a polluted area but both places have air that is suitable for us to breathe and keeps us ticking along.

Air is at once a gentle breeze on a warm day that we appreciate for the coolness it gives us. Air is also destructive, like a howling tornado tearing buildings apart. It can be an icy wind that chills us to the bone or it can be the soothing words whispered to us by the voice of our lover. Air is fantastic, it makes us live, we commune with air all the time.

Breathe deeply and think of how wonderful it is to breathe in air that is keeping you alive every minute of every day. Before you move on to working with Air, read through the associations and come up with a list of your own.

Magical Associations

Wicca places Air in the East quarter of the circle, it is associated with dawn and the season of spring.

Tools we use connected with air are feathers, smudge and incense, bells, aromatherapy, chanting, sound, fans, songs, poetry and the mind.

Air colours are pale gray, white, blue and yellow.

Air astrology signs are Gemini, Libra and Aquarius.

Air elemental spirits are called Sylphs and mystical air creatures include Pegasus, the griffon, dragonflies, bees and birds.

Magical spells using air can include those done for birth, beginnings, creativity, clear thinking, prophetic dreams, helping with mental and intellectual matters, studying and exams, divination and starting new projects, inviting new things or situations into your life.

Working with Air

To cleanse yourself thoroughly with air, you can use a smudge bundle made of home-grown sage or an incense stick with a spray of feathers to waft the lovely scent all over you and remove grime from your aura. You could use the incense or feathers alone or you could use a rattle or a bell to let the sound vibrate in the air around you and remove any negative energy and balance your aura. Try singing different notes or hum to make the air around you vibrate away any energy that is sticking to you after your day.

Or you could find the purest air you can get near to and go for a walk in that area, being conscious of the air. Breathe it in with the intention of clearing your mind from all stress and problems. Walking is relaxing and meditative and combining that with the intention of breathing in cleanliness and breathing out stress is good for the soul.

Cleansing can also be done by blowing away energy, directing your breath to nudge away anything you don't need.

Think about how you would create a circle using air. It could look like a swirling mass of feathers, meshing together to form the sphere or a multitude of gentle honeybees buzzing around the perimeter to stop energy escaping. Perhaps a circle made of air would be an iridescent barrier made of giant dragonfly wings.

Use your breath to breathe the magic circle into being. Walk round the circle and blowing air into place, asking that it create a barrier to hold your magic energy, state that this circle of air is a sacred space where you can explore the mysteries of air. Imagine the air building up into the circle, visualise it full of feathers or swirls of air colours or clouds.

Having cast the circle, invoke the elements and when you come to air, think clearly on inviting the qualities of air to your ritual. Ask the God and Goddess to be present.

Now sit quietly and take some time to relax, thinking and breathing air. Meditate on all the things that air brings to you, all the qualities it has that you use in your life or would like to use more of. Air can provide a steady flow of mental energy and a swift breeze to blow away the cobwebs of stale emotions or ideas. Air is inspirational and creative. Think about what air means to you, not what you read about air in a book, including this one. Make notes if you want to be able to recall your thoughts clearly later on, although thoughts belong to air so it should be easy.

Think of something new you want to create, some plans you want to set in motion. Use the examples below to create your own spell to help see how essential air can be for magic.

To raise power for your desire, again having a key word to sum up the desired outcome, begin to chant or intone as you breathe in and out. Maybe you could use a bell to send vibrations of air into the cone. Every time you breath in, imagine you are drawing in powerful air energy and on the exhalation you can direct your breath into the cone of swirling energy. Visualise the cone of power as a miniature whirlwind, scooping up energy as it spins round and round, finally shout your keyword and feel your breath as you do so, forcing the air up and out the top of the cone, releasing it into the universe.

Visualise the energy shooting out onto the strands of the web and returning to you in the form of your desired outcome.

Ground yourself and be aware of how an air ritual compares to that of earth.

Consecrate some food and drink with air themes – meringues, sponge cakes, sparkling water. Offer some to the Old Ones and close the circle in the reverse order as normal, seeing the air of the circle blowing away all around you and returning to the general space surrounding you. Write down any images or intuitions that came to you during the ritual.

Air Spells

Air magic includes spells for birth, beginnings, new initiatives, starting things, travel, inviting people or circumstances into your life, healing of the mind, clarity of thought, children and babies, decision making, exams and interviews, form filling and legal matters, communication, change, divination and dreams.

Sound: use a whistle, flute, drum, clapping hands or some other instrument (you don't have to play it well, just get it to make a sound). Think of something you want to achieve and draw this in the air with your wand or finger, really visualise it being there, just hanging in the air. Now take your instrument and play softly, letting the vibrations wash over the words, play gradually louder and with the intention of making those words float away on the air to bring about your wish. As the music (or cacophony) gets louder give one last blast on the instrument and see the words shoot off to do your will.

Decisions: if you have a decision that you are continually fretting over, give it to the birds. Bake some bread or biscuits while thinking of the different choices and when the baking is ready, crumble it outside somewhere for the birds to eat (if you don't have a garden try a local park, riverside or churchyard). Speak aloud or quietly and ask the spirit of air to give you an answer. Invite the birds to the feast. Wait until at least one bird has come to eat and see which direction it flies away in, (decide beforehand if left or right means 'yes'). If no birds come to the feast, this could be a sign of your unease about the choice you have made and suggests the decision was not the right one for you. Whatever the outcome, however you interpret the results, it will give you a clearer idea of where your heart lies and that will tell you which choice you really want to make.

Communication: to ease communication between you and another person, you will need a sheet of yellow paper, scissors, pencil, sellotape. Take a piece of paper and draw a line down the middle, now draw a picture of yourself on one side of the line and of the person you are having communication difficulties with on the other side. The line represents the barrier or arguments between you. Fold the paper in half so the pictures meet each other face-on. Cut out a thin slice along the centre of the paper, cutting away the line between you. Open it out again and sellotape the paper up the middle, bringing the two figures closer together and without a line between them. While you are doing all of this, state that you are removing all obstacles between you and that communication will be easier from now on. Now breathe deeply, blow at the space between the two figures to clear the air and state that you are willing to talk to them and resolve the issues without waiting for them to come to you and without erecting the barrier again. Ask for the air to be cleared between you.

Balloons: fill these with air and use for a variety of reasons. You can bash them about and pop them to get rid of anger or grief, fill a helium balloon and release it to send loving thoughts and healing energy to a loved one far away. To get back something you've lost, write it on paper tied to the balloon and state that as the balloon finds its way across the skies so the object will find its way back to you.

Feathers: can be woven into a dream catcher to bring pleasant dreams and stop nightmares and worry from keeping you awake at night. Dream catchers are easy to make, get a large stiff circular thing - a bracelet, embroidery hoop, bend a branch into a circle – and wind it randomly with wool or cotton in any pattern across the hoop that you find pleasing, tie feathers into it and let it hang above your bed to bring sweet dreams.

Kites: on a windy day, get a silver ribbon to represent successful results in some academic or intellectual venture and tie it to a kite string. As the kite flies high, picture your success and the form it will take – a degree certificate or the right decision being reached in court for example. As the ribbon flickers in the wind, ask for the God and Goddess of the skies to hear your plea and bring about a successful conclusion. Charge it with magical energy to give it greater power.

Air Spirits

To meet with air spirits, the Sylphs, we need to spend time getting to know air in the real world. Go to lots of different places and plenty of usual places. Everywhere you go, breathe with the intention of finding out about air. This should not be hard – after all, you are breathing now. What is that breath like? Cold, warm, room temperature? Are you breathing fast, shallow, deep or slow. Notice how the air smells in different places and at different times of the day and night. Become aware of how not only the air changes, but how our breathing changes also, depending on what we are doing.

After an hour in the gym we can smell sweat, our own and that of other people, when we return to the changing room. This air, and the depth of our breathing, differs greatly to the air we breathe when we go for a walk through suburban parks and this is different again to the air of the seaside. Our reactions to air are often unnoticeable but it does show how sensitive we are to air and also how easily we can both enhance and pollute our air.

Take time to listen to the air, is it blowing fast or slow? Is it cold or warm, angry, calm or indifferent? Ask a question and see if air gives you some kind of answer, whispering through leaves or gently stirring against your face. See if any air creatures, dragonflies or birds, are present and see if you can pick up any feelings or intuitions from them regarding your question. After spending time with air in the present world, try going on a journey to meet with an air spirit.

Follow the normal routes and routines for visiting your place of power and see what the air is like there before you do anything else.

Ask for your guardian or guide to appear to you, greet him/her and tell them what you have done since your last meeting – did you act on any of the things the earth spirits told you for example?

Ask your guardian to take you to a place where you can meet with an air elemental. Follow your guide along springtime paths to the early morning land of Air.

When your guide disappears, ask an Air spirit to come to you and as you wait, be aware of the air all round you. The Air spirit may come to you as a particular bird – hawk, eagle, sparrow, or as an insect, a mosquito or ladybird, or it may come to you as a cloud or a swirling bunch of wind-stirred leaves. Speak with the sylph and spend time getting to know the spirit of Air, asking questions and giving answers, feeling with each of your senses what air can do for you.

When you return, give your thanks to the spirit and ask if there is anything it needs from you.

Now call your guardian and go back to your place of power. Offer thanks and blessings to the quarters and return slowly to the 'normal' world. Have something to eat and drink, keeping some as an offering to the birds and flying insects.

Make sure you feel fully grounded before getting up and going about your ordinary business. If you are not grounded properly, try holding some quartz crystal or stamp your feet around. You can breathe energy up into yourself if you feel weak or let excess energy drain away to the ground if you feel light-headed.

Fire

Natural fire comes to us in different ways. Lightning that crashes through the sky, belting through and discharging electricity into the earth. Volcanic eruptions, violently spewing out hot streams of fire, melting, flowing, creeping, the volcano is a destroyer, covering everything in its path with larva and burning it up. Hot springs, heated by underground sources of fire or volcanoes, are warm pools in which we can bathe or hot geysers that send boiling water shooting into the sky. Forest fires, extreme dry conditions and an excess of heat can trigger the consuming flames that can rage for days or weeks.

Fire is naturally destructive. Mankind, however, has tamed it, to a certain degree. We can use fire to create and transform.

We can dig a pit to contain an outdoor fire as a source of heat, a soft glow of light and as a cooking tool. We can light candles and torches to illuminate dark nights. We can bake and cook delicious food that would be indigestible otherwise. We can use fire to heat our homes and workplaces. We use a spark of fire in the combustion chambers of the vehicles we use to transport us. We can strengthen clay pots by putting them in a furnace. A blacksmith can protect a horse's hooves and create elaborate metal work in her forge. We can cremate our dead. We incinerate our waste, despite the carcinogenic fumes this gives out. We use fire to keep our power stations running and we use its electricity in the majority of our activities.

Fire represents our deep desires, our angers, our loves and passions. Fire is our creative energy, our inner flame of power and action. Fire gives us raging emotions and burning desire, courage and strength. Fire has become our tool and has been with us for thousands of years. Without fire to keep us warm and heat our food, how would we modern humans survive?

Fire has been essential to us for many thousands of years and as such it is natural that we should welcome its power into our magic. Fire is about action, energy and movement. Fire as it relates to Wicca is the energy that makes us persevere, it is our determination to charge on with things and get the job done.

Magical Associations
Fire is situated in the South, coinciding with mid-summer and noon.

It is the God, rather than the Goddess, who is most commonly associated with Fire, as God of the Sun. The Egyptian God Ra is a Sun God, and the Holly King and Oak King represent the waxing and waning of the solar year.

Fire is connected to our energy, creative and destructive, and represents our passions, anger and love.

The astrological signs associated with fire are Aries, Leo and Sagittarius.

The Wiccan tools of fire are candles, the athame (in some traditions), amber and other red/orange crystals, volcanic rock.

Fire elementals are called Salamanders and mythical, magical fire creatures are the phoenix, the lion and dragons.

Colours of fire are orange, red, gold, yellow, sunset and sunrise colours.

Fire in magic is used to remove anger and harness its energy for good, to bring happiness and money, to get rid of things, to bring creative energy.

Working with Fire

It is possible to completely rejuvenate the aura and persona in about five minutes with fire. Small cake candles work best for this ritual as they don't take long to burn down and it is nice to be able to use all of the candle's energy without having to extinguish it.

Set a birthday cake candle on a saucer and light it. Put your hands near the flame, palms facing each other around the flame and see the golden glow the flame instantly sends to your skin. Feel that warmth and imagine it is soaking into your skin, filling your hands with warm, healing energy. This is instant magic, you can tell it is working by the warmth and the glow of the fire element on your hands.

As you feel the warmth and see the golden light cascading onto your hands, use your mind to draw it into you, filling your palms with energy. Wait until you have lots of energy then place both palms on the site of your root chakra, transferring the energy directly to your aura's power spot. Repeat the process, warm and glowing, energy building up in the palms (which, incidentally, have power spots, mini chakras, all of their own), transferring the energy to the sacral chakra. Work your way up through the chakras until you come to the crown. Now gather more of the energy and give it to your feet. By now, the candle will be almost completely burned so use up the last of the energy and give it to any part of your body that feels stiff or sick, or gather it up and channel it into your aura by way of the root chakra.

This exercise is especially beneficial if you are feeling run down or depressed. It is useful for newcomers to the craft as it shows the magic at work; you really do have a golden aura, warm hands and you can physically put this warmth on other parts of the body and feel the benefits.

Working with fire does present a particular danger and this is the foremost consideration when a ritual focuses entirely on fire. Not only do we have one or two candles as normal during ritual, but we are specifically invoking fire into our rite and you will probably want to use more candles than you can shake a stick at. So please, be safety conscious. No flowing skirts or draping sleeves and place an emergency bucket of water next to the altar. Thank you.

Prepare yourself and make your sacred space. As you cast the circle, imagine the energy coming from your fingertips (athame etc) as a stream of red, orange and gold ribbons being blown like flames in a breeze or see the sphere forming as a barrier made out of phoenix feathers or shining brightly like gold armour plating.

Fire is located in the South of the circle, but where is your source of fire right now? Try invoking the element of fire in the place where your fire actually is, an altar candle in the north or a central fire pit for outdoor rituals. You could still invoke the presence of the guardians in the South quarter if you wish to.

Invoke each element, focusing on the essence of earth and air and then conjure your thoughts and knowledge about fire and bring this into your invocation with the other elements in turn.

Ask for the presence of the Goddess and the God as the Sun King and settle into a comfortable position for some time spent in reflection and meditation on the element of fire. What do you think of first in connection with fire? Think about how often you use fire and what you use it for, imagine yourself being warmed by a real fire and stare into the flames, imagine the flickering and crackling. Think of the fiery energy, the passionate states of emotion like anger and heated desire.

Fire spells are related to love, happiness, anger, money, desire and transformation. We do fire magic to help transform anger to positive action, to bring us light in our darkest hours or to bring us love. Think of a fire aspect and a situation you know of that would benefit from fire's energy. Come up with one or two words to sum up the goal you want to achieve and create a spell using your intuitive guesses or ideas from the list below. Alternatively, make it up as you go along, keeping your focus clear and concise.

To raise energy for your spell with the element of fire, you need to move, to feel the passion you have for your goal. Dance your desire, shout your goals. As you feel the energy building, visualise the cone of power as a roaring bonfire and see the natural shape of the fire forming the peak of the cone.

When you feel the energy is peaking, let it go with all your passion sending it forwards onto the web of wyrd.

Now step back and ground yourself. Meditate on the altar candles to bring your awareness and focus to the present.

Have some fiery food on your altar, chunks of sweet red peppers, a bowl of chilli, ginger snap biscuits and some fiery or fire coloured drink like orange, mead or red wine.

Ask the Sun God and the Goddess to honour your magic and bid them hail and farewell. Give thanks to the element of fire and the other elements in turn. Ground yourself thoroughly and write up notes about your thoughts and feelings when dealing with fire magic and compare this to your notes on earth and air.

Fire Spells

We can use the destructive force of fire to get rid of things. Write down something you want to get rid of, a bad habit say, and burn the paper in a flame, stating that as the paper burns it destroys the thing you want to get rid of, leaving space for positive energy to enter your life. Again, do this with the Wiccan ethics of positive intentions only.

We can use fire to create things in our kitchen. If you are feeling low or blue, add some consecrated and charged spices to your food with the intention that it fills you up with happy, golden energy. Create a feast for others through the element of fire and hold a party, a guaranteed way of cheering yourself up.

Fire magic is done for love. To bring more love into you life, it is important to realise that love starts on the inside. You need to love yourself. This is hard, but fire can help us. Take a red candle, carve your name into it together with words that represent how you would like to feel about yourself, love, passion, kind, energetic, enthusiastic, serene, attractive, beautiful, creative, talented, loving. Light the candle and as the flame burns, ask fire to help you love yourself, take in the orangey light and warmth and know that you are a wonderful and unique person with qualities that make you loveable and loving. Love yourself.

Fire is transforming, we can transform our anger into creative energy. Think of something that has made you angry recently, visualise it as a blazing bonfire, huge and roaring. Try to visualise the fire shrinking down, concentrating its heat and flames into a smaller and smaller fire. Let the fire, and with it your anger, reduce further down until it is a tiny ball of intense flame. Imagine how powerful it is, all that stored up anger and heat, intense and specific. Allow yourself to pick it up, knowing that it belongs to you and cannot harm you. Now think of something positive you can channel it into that relates to the issue you were angry about and hold the fire close to your heart. Picture very clearly both the anger condensed into a ball and the things you would prefer to spend your energy on. Now let the anger out as a laser, shooting out of the ball until all the flames and anger are used up. Direct the energy towards the positive aim and release it into the universe. Ask for the elements of fire to transform your anger into positive action.

Fire is protective, our ancestors lit fires through the night to keep away predators and we can do something similar. Let's suppose you want to protect your house from burglary while on holiday. Draw a picture of your house along with any symbols or words you feel will sum up the type of protection you want to get, general protection, home security, repel thieves. The pentagram is a protective symbol and so are some runes, so you might want to do some research into relevant runes and include these. Have some red cloth, red cotton and needle ready in your circle and begin to sew the cloth around the paper, closing it in. With every stitch repeat a protective mantra such as my home is safe while I am away. Consecrate this with the element of fire, hang it above your front door and ask for the fire elementals, maybe in the form of a fire-breathing dragon, to watch over and protect your home while you are away.

Fire Spirits

Fire elementals are salamanders and we can only truly connect with them when live fire is present. A candle is a safe way to connect with fire indoors, but there is nothing better than sitting by an outdoor fire circle, staring into the flames and being warmed by them.

Night is the best time to meet with nature spirits of fire, as they are more visible at this time. Sit by a roaring fire, stare into the flames. They are hypnotic, changing, moving, living, sparking, blue, orange, yellow, golden. Fire makes our skin glow golden, makes us warm. Feel the energy of the fire, try to make out patterns or shapes in the flames. Watch a piece of wood and see how the fire changes and moves along the wood as it burns.

See if you are affected by the fire, perhaps it alters your mood, energises you or makes you inwardly reflective and meditative. It is common to find yourself drifting into an almost trance-like, hypnogogic state. Go with this feeling, relax into it and float along with whatever images or suggestions come to you in the images created by the flames.

Give thanks to the fire spirits for showing you their nature and make an offering by throwing some of your food into the fire. Feed the fire spirits and hear the rush of flames in thanks as the offering is consumed.

When you know about physical aspects of fire and have talked with fire in the real world, you are ready to go on a sacred journey to meet the spirits of fire.

Carry out your cleansing and chakra exercises. Create your sacred space in the physical world and cast a circle, invoking every element and the Goddess and God.

Use the deep relaxation techniques to get into the journey state and meet your guardian in the place of power. Ask your guide to take you to meet with fire and follow your instincts in connecting with that wild, elemental being.

The fire elemental might talk with you from the fiery pit of a volcano as you stand safely on the edge, or it might come to you as being of shimmering light, or a shining star.

Find out if fire needs anything from you, if you need more fire energy or less in your life. Fire can help with passions, anger, creativity and energy. Ask the fire elements if they can help you with any issues you have surrounding those things and listen carefully to their advice.

If you have a drummer or drumming tape which beats out the rapid, broken call-back signal, this is the time to ask your guide to lead you back to the place of power and from there travel back to the ordinary levels of consciousness. If you are not using drums, then come back when you have finished talking with fire.

Make notes on all that you learned in the realm of fire.

Close your circle, offering thanks to the elements and deity. Ground yourself and offer a token of gratitude to fire, giving away gold coins or jewellery to charity would be one way of doing this.

Water

The element of water is not only essential for the health and well-being of all life on our planet, it is also essential to combat and balance the other elements. Fire and water combined become steam, which we can turn into sources of energy or use in a sauna. Water and earth, combined with light (fire) make our plants grow. When fire gets out of hand, we use water to stop its destruction and only water can restore the dry, baked earth of drought-ridden land to productive and fertile use once more.

Earth is sometimes referred to as the blue planet because of the vast amount water, seas and oceans, on its surface. Our bodies are around 80% water, it comes out of our pores when we sweat, we drink water to nourish us and bathe in it to make ourselves clean. We use water to grow our crops, we travel in boats and ships on the surface of our seas and rivers. Most cultures eat fish, the ultimate in water spirits made flesh.

Waterfalls can be used to generate electricity and turn the cogs and wheels in a mill to grind grains for flour. Water on the earth's surface evaporates and forms clouds which become heavy and rain on the earth, starting the cycle again. Water can lap gently at the side of a child's paper boat or fiercely twirl so fast it drags anything in its current down a vortex into the depths of the ocean. It can crash and hurl at the pier, flood our homes and still provide us with a calming influence if we look into the still waters of a deep lake.

We can become healthy as we exercise by swimming and rowing through water. Animals have diverse reactions to water; cats detest getting wet, dogs adore splashing in water, beavers thrive and live in water and most children hate having a bath but love water fights with pump-action water-pistols.

Magical Associations

Water is normally invoked in the West quarter of the circle, relating to autumn and twilight.

Water deities are the sea Gods Poseidon and Neptune, Goddess of the sea Yemaya, and in addition, Selene and Diana, as moon Goddesses, would be congenial to water rituals.

Water's elemental spirits are the Undines, or Ondines. Other watery creatures include frogs and toads, dolphins, seals, fish and mystical water beasts like mermaids, selkies, kelpies and the loch ness monster.

The tools of water are water itself, the chalice or cup, the scrying bowl, and mirrors.

Astrological signs of water are Cancer, Scorpio and Pisces.

Generally seen as the element of the emotions and balance, water can bring calming energy and peace to fraught situations and can wash away unwanted problems.

Water is also associated with the moon and science tells us that the tides of the sea are pulled by the force of the moon's gravity.

Water is connected with our blood and women's menstrual cycles and women will often be more emotionally and psychically sensitive during their menses.

Water colours are all shades of blue, white and sometimes gray or green.

Working with Water

We can use water in obvious ways to prepare ourselves mentally for rituals through taking a lavender bath to relax us or drinking ginger tea to energise us, or simply through showering or washing our hands as we cleanse ourselves.

Water can be used to cast the circle by sprinkling it around the circumference as you channel energy to form the sphere.

A circle boundary cast with water can be seen as a blue, foamy, swishing energy, as a water fall, gushing round the circle or as any other water images that you want to use. Be inventive and imaginative.

It makes sense when an element is physically present to go to it in its natural position so you if you are lucky enough to be outdoors with a stream in the east, then your water, for the purpose of the ritual is in the east, not west. You can still invoke the guardians of the west in addition the elements of water. Invoke the other elements and the God and Goddess of water. Sit in your circle with a glass or bowl of water in front of you, break the surface with your finger tips, place some on your forehead or drink some. Reflect on what water means to you, how you use it and what qualities it has. We survive by utilising water but also have water of our own in the form of sweat, blood and tears. What does water contribute to your life and how do you relate to the multiple aspects of water?

Water magic is needed to bring balance to our emotions, but that is not always easy in our society. From an early age, we are taught, especially for men, that crying is a weakness and must be done in private. Consider the last time you saw someone express grief in public and the reactions of the people around them. Pull yourself together. Come on, it's all right. A pat on the back and being told to stop crying in case people see is the opposite of what we need when we are upset. Similarly, we rarely follow our instincts to jump up and down and shout out loud with joy when we are happy, again it's a case of worrying about what other people might think. But other people are just like us, they have emotions too. Is the real reason we have to hide our emotions because other people fear their emotions may be brought out in the open if they come face to face with tears or joyful abandon?

To bring your emotions into balance is to express, without fear (or with it, fear is after all one of our emotions), all of our emotions to the full. This ritual is designed to bring that emotion out into the open and to express it as fully as you can. It is worth finding a partner or friend to work through this ritual with, it does not need to be another Wiccan, just someone who can be there to comfort you or share your laughter if necessary. We need to feel ready for this type of work in order for it work successfully. If you are not feeling up to this, then do some other type of water magic before closing your circle.

Think about something that recently made you feel happy or sad, calm or panic-stricken. Focus clearly on that situation. Recall the moment when you first found out about the circumstances that contributed to the fear/excitement. Write it down on a sheet of paper and underneath list all the feelings that it brought up.

Now stare at your reflection in a mirror and tell yourself that it is all right to have these emotions. Call them out one by one, each time accepting the emotion. Fear, relief, regret, anger, worry, concern, humour, elatedness, bliss, lust, happiness, delight, pleasure, terror, sorrow.

Look into your eyes in the mirror and say it again. I love myself. I accept my emotions. I am happy, I am sad, I am sorry. Be honest with yourself, open up and let your tears flow or your smile turn to outright laughter.

As you start to physically feel any type of emotions, including those unrelated to the situation you initially thought of, start to draw energy into your aura from the ground through your root chakra. Let it come into your body, up to your chest and out through your hands. Breathe in deeply as you pull energy into your outstretched hands, feel it as a ball and visualise your emotion sitting in that ball. Hold it up for the water God and Goddess. Ask them to bless your emotions and help you feel your emotions with honesty and abandon, free from fear, in future.

Lower the emotional energy in the ball and squash it down into the bowl of water in front of you. Immerse your hands in the water to transfer all of the energy and then drink the water with the clear intention of drinking-in and owning all your feelings.

If you are feeling emotional, joyful or tearful, after this ritual, it is important not to prematurely stifle your feelings, especially for the sake of others. If you have someone with you, talk about how you feel and discuss the situation you were originally thinking of.

It can be hard to say that you love and accept yourself, especially when confronted with yourself in a mirror, so don't be put off if you can't face it yet. Keep working at this from time to time and see how much easier it becomes.

When you are ready, pick up the piece of paper and call out the emotions a final time, giving thanks to yourself for accepting and expressing them.

You can keep the paper in a secret place, bury or compost it or use rice paper and tear it into tiny pieces to feed the water birds in your nearest river.

Finish the ritual by consecrating natural watery or juicy foods such as melon, sea kale, oranges and more water to drink.

Give thanks to the water spirits and elements, to the Goddess and God and close your circle.

Grounding is especially important after this type of emotional work and going for a brisk walk can work well as it gives you exercise, fresh air and time to absorb and reflect on the ritual.

Water Spells

Wicca always has something secreted up its sleeve and it should be apparent by now that the elements have more to offer than would at first seem to be the case. Water can shock us, if a cloud breaks suddenly on a hot, sunny day and throws torrents of rain at us, for example and cold water splashed on your face early in the morning brings you wide awake.

Bathing with appropriate herbs and oils in the water can be healing, calming or energising depending on the scents used and the intention. Chamomile or lavender are good for soothing and relaxing, bringing calmness to a stressful situation, rosemary can help to bring healing to tired muscles and both ginger and peppermint will stimulate and energise your senses.

Water can be good fun too – set up imaginary targets in your garden and give them the names of things or people you feel angry about. Now fill a water-pistol and fire away, aiming at your targets, not as a way of harming them, but as a way of releasing your tension and frustration. (This can be done under the guise of water-fights with your children if you have curious neighbours.)

Water is life-giving and can liven up a dull situation, although you should be clear about what kind of excitement you are looking for. Consecrate a jug or bowl of water in a magic circle, bless it in the name of the God and Goddess. Now draw energy up from your roots, through all your chakra points and let it fill your aura. Hold your hands face down over the water and let the energy come through the energy centres in your palms and flow into the water. Bottle the magically charged water and leave it outside or on a windowsill for the three days of a full moon, asking the Goddess to give it further power. Drink the water, a little each day, until it is gone and see what begins to stir in your life.

Scrying is a simple method of divination using water or mirrors. Take a dark coloured bowl and fill it with water. Your working space should be lit only by a single candle. Cast a circle and consecrate the water, with a candle on the other side of the bowl from you. Think clearly of what you want to know about your future or what other people are getting up to in your absence. Stare into the water and ask your questions. Information can come as images or colours on the water's surface or as internal thoughts which give you the answers you seek. Be patient, you may find it takes practice, not only to see any pictures but also to interpret them. Some people can see images in washing up water as this is quite a boring, mundane task, requiring little input and leaving the mind free to wander.

Water can take things away from us in the currents of rivers and streams. Take a piece of rice paper (this is natural, biodegradable matter so it does not harm the environment), write on it whatever you want to be rid of in your life. Fold it into a paper boat or tear into pieces and place the paper in the current of a stream, asking water to take the situation away from you. Watch it drift away and out of your life. Affirm that you will no longer give your thoughts or energy to the situation and find something new to fill the void it will leave.

Another way of using water is to get rid of anger and a specific water spell for anger is to take a stone or pebble and channel your anger into it then hurl it as hard as you can into the currents of a fast flowing, deep river. Ask the water sprites to take the anger away and recycle its energy.

Water beetles such as whirligigs and pond skaters can help with magic too and give us direction when making decisions. Go to a pond and sit still so the creatures can get used to your presence. Ask your question silently and wait for the water spirits to manifest your answer. Maybe a toad or newt will appear, perhaps a group of whirligigs will suddenly move to the left or right. See if this relates to your question in some way, give thanks to the water creatures before you leave.

Water Spirits

We find water in diverse places in nature and it is natural water that can give us the best insights into the nature of water's sprites. Go on a quest to visit as many natural sources of water as you can. This could be done over several days or months if necessary. Water can be found as rivers, streams and gentle brooks, ditches and dykes through farmland, waterfalls, springs and wells, ponds, lakes and rain. Go swimming or walk your dog in a gentle shower.

Visit these places and spend as much time as you can in them. Each time you try and connect with the water spirits in the natural environment, look for physical signs of them stirring the water's surface. Water animals are all types of fish, frogs, toads and newts, water insects and birds, dolphins, jellyfish, sea urchins and seals. It might not seem spiritually attractive to sit by a stagnant lake in the throws of a torrential downpour but if you dress appropriately, it needn't be as miserable as you think and will help you understand that all aspects of water are vital to the survival of all earth's creatures. Think about how water can affect you and also how you can affect water, in terms of water usage and waste water. If you spend any length of time by rocky shores which seals are known to frequent, it won't be long before you see one. Seals are considered to be especially magical and they enter into an old, old story.

In times gone by, a lonely fisherman decided to find himself a wife and sitting by the sea one night at the full moon, he saw a group of seals take off their seal skins to become beautiful women. He took his boat out and stole one of the skins left lying on the rocks while the women bathed. Back on dry land, the fisherman hid the skin in a box in the attic of his little house. The seal women returned to the rocks and stepped into their skins to become seals once more. The seal-woman whose skin had been stolen came to the fisherman, asking him to return it. He refused and forced her to live with him as his wife. Before long, she bore him a son and as the child grew, he wondered why his mother was so drawn to the sea, as she would sit for hours staring longingly at the lapping waves. She told him about her life as a seal and the next day, when his father took the fishing boat out to sea, the boy searched the house until he found the hidden seal skin. The woman took the skin and kissed her son farewell. She swam out to the rocks and put on the seal skin, returning to the water she had missed so dreadfully. Her seal folk came to greet her and bobbed their heads at the boy. Every full moon, they would still gather on the rocks to become human for a night, but from that time onwards, one seal would remain on the rocks as a guardian of the precious seal skins.

This is a story about transformation, home and belonging. If a seal makes itself known to you, think of what is shows you. Does it tell you anything about your own cycles of transformation and your true place of belonging? Think of what water can teach you and ask the water spirits to help you learn about water. Giving thanks to water can be done by way of clearing litter out of natural water sources and feeding water birds in the middle of winter or giving a donation to a sea-life sanctuary.

Water journeys can be done during the time of the full moon to enhance the experience and connection with water.

Cast a circle as normal and do some deep relaxation exercises to prompt you into the journey state. As you gain experience in journeying, you will find you do not always need to follow the rainbow coloured meditations to get into the necessary state of mind, but can slip gently into journey by relaxation alone. Try this now and revert back to the colours if you find it contributes to a deeper journey state.

Start in your place of power and ask your guide to take you to a safe space where you can meet a water spirit. Watch carefully as you wait for the spirit. It might appear as a water nymph or mermaid, perhaps a newt or a dolphin. Talk with the water spirit about how water can help you in your life and ask if there is anything water needs from you.

Give thanks when you are ready or at a signal if you are using drums. Make notes on your journey and close down your sacred space.

Ground yourself by drinking clear, cool water and eating something earthy such as granary bread.

Compare your notes on all of the four physical elements before you move on to connect with spirit.

Do you connect more deeply with earth or fire, air or water? Some people are drawn to one particular element and this often corresponds to their astrological sign.

Spirit

Spirit is not seen as an element in the same sense as the other four, as it has no physical manifestation that we can recognise. It is the energy that binds all the others together. It works as a catalyst, igniting the other elements into action. Spirit is the life-force that exists in every living thing and every non-living thing, from rocks to plants to people. It is the energy which connects us with everything else, it is our anchor to reality and yet it transcends this reality and exists throughout all the worlds.

Spirit is the essence of life, our souls, our life force. It is what makes us tick and is all around us and within us at all times. Magic is about working with spirit by communicating what we want to happen and then raising and directing energy to bring it about.

We describe people as having high spirits, being low in spirits or being spirited. This is because on a deep subconscious level, we are aware of how spirit moves within that person. We sense that people with a sunny, bright disposition have a different type of spiritual energy within them than someone who becomes depressed or downhearted easily.

Whenever we do any form of magic, we are using spirit, life energy, to connect with the spirits of other people and things to help us achieve our goals. For example, healing magic sends energy to help the spirit of the ill person to recover, it gives them strength.

Working with Spirit

We use spirit every time we cast a circle and raise energy. When you sense auras it is spirit that you are connecting with.

The web of life, the spider web of connections, can be seen as a representation of how spirit connects and binds every aspect of life. To see this in action, try the following exercise.

Think of someone you really like whom you have not seen for a few weeks and now wish to contact. Focus on them very clearly – looking at a photograph of them will help your concentration. Think about the connection you have with that person, how they make you smile or laugh, the way they make you feel. Try and summon up the emotional link between you and them. Draw energy up through your aura and pass it over their photograph, ask them to contact you. Now visualise a strand of the web with you at one end and them on the other, draw up more energy and begin to send it pulsing along the web of life. See this as a bright white light that grows bigger and flows faster towards them. Continue to visualise this energy and the connection between you for a while, all the time focusing on them contacting you.

Now stop the energy flow, see the last of it go to them and ground yourself. Put the photograph away and wait for them to get in touch. You need to change your belief that this will work into a knowledge that you have made it work already. You will normally find this exercise works within a couple of days - the telephone rings or you bump into your friend in the street unexpectedly.

Spirit is said to lie in the centre of the circle, but really it is the circle. Spirit is called in to make us aware of the universal energy which makes magic possible. We can bend it, shape it, give it form and let it go.

This is a spell casting to create a thought-form which can be programmed or charged with a set of instructions to carry out. Thought-forms are a very strong presence of energy that can add weight to our own energy and nudge others round to our way of thinking. Thought-forms can be raised for any number of reasons, such as the thought-form of a fierce dog who walks alongside you to protect you in unsavoury places, giving off vibrations and energies that deter maliciousness away from you. A thought-form can be a tiger to watch over your home while you are away or it can take the form of a far-flying swallow to carry messages or dreams to a loved one who is far away.

Cast a circle with the usual invocations and think of a friend who needs energy for something, recovery from illness or settling a dispute with an employer for example. If the energy needed to help them were an animal, what would it be? The strength of a lion (fire) can help with confidence problems, a bird (air) can represent communication or freedom, a bull (earth) will give determination and will power, a crab (water) might be appropriate for anyone needing to defend themselves against injustice. The most important thing for this spell, as with everything in Wicca, is that you choose something by using your intuition and your own ideas about what would be helpful. If you think of lions as a destructive force because they eat other animals, you would not want to send that energy to your friend in order to help them so come up with an alternative that you find meaningful.

Choose an animal and begin to raise energy by pulling it into your working space from the ground, the sky and the space around you. Grab handfuls of energy and collect it into a ball. Start to shape it into the form of your chosen animal, moulding the energy with your hands and your thoughts. Make it feel as realistic as you can, give it wings, legs, fur, scales or feathers. Give it a mouth, eyes and ears (it must at least have the ability to hear).

Now hold this thought-form animal up to your mouth and whisper to it. Tell it exactly what you want it to do for your friend.

Take this energy to Janine and give her the willpower to stand up for her right to a fair salary.

Ask the animal to wait with you as you raise energy in a cone of power. When the power reaches a peak, send the animal off with it as it whooshes up out of the apex. Concentrate on the energies you want to develop during this spell casting, focus on helping your friend with the energy and animal used. See the thought-form flowing along the web, or rather, see it flying, swimming, running or leaping until it reaches them. Imagine it settling down beside them as a protector, advisor or guardian.

Close your circle and give thanks in whatever way you feel would be of benefit to the animal you called to your aid. Next time you see your friend, see if the thought-form energy is discernible.

All successful magic is done with the same principles of using spirit to make the connections necessary for attaining our goals. Providing you are putting your will power into the spell, you do not need any tools whatsoever and if you are not putting your will power into it then no amount of tools will make your magic work.

9

Environmental Activism

I am Gaia, this I say
Look to the future
Look to the day
When the wolves cannot howl
When the tigers cannot hunt
When all the birds are silent
When all the flowers – picked
When all the tribes are civilized
When all the rain is acid
When all the trees are felled
When all the whales – gone.
When all the land is concrete
When all the sea is black
When all the air – polluted.
When all the crops – mutated
When all the water – tainted
When all the people raped.
When the seed will not grow
When the cattle will not breed
When the sun does not warm
When the storm does not end
When all the passion – dulled
When all the caring – ended
When all the summer – chilled
When all the earth is killed.
It does not have to be this way
Look to the future,
Look to the day -
I am Gaia, this I say.

As well as thinking about and connecting with the spiritual aspects of each element, as Wiccans we should also concern ourselves with the physical reality of what is happening to the earth.

As humans, we do not always treat the earth we live on with respect or honour. We degrade the earth in many ways, through clear-cut tree felling, toxic land-fill sites, destruction of natural environments through pollution, road-building and urban expansion. Animals are killed for their meat and skins, they are experimented upon, abused and used. Precious minerals, oils and gases are extracted from the earth for human consumption, turned into chemicals and petroleum derivatives that affect every aspect of our lives. Even the ancient sacred sites and standing stone circles are under almost continual pressure and constant threat of being knocked down, built around or exploited.

Air is essential to us and yet we continue to pollute it every day. The incidence of childhood asthma and animals with respiratory disorders (dogs and cats being far closer to car fumes than adults), is increasing every year. Incinerators burn up our waste products and release cancer-causing dioxins and toxins into the atmosphere, nuclear radiation causes birth defects and cancers, smoking cigarettes is proven to be life-threatening even to those who do not smoke. Our water, land and food are being polluted with waste chemicals from factories and pesticides, insecticides and herbicides from monoculture farming. Our bodily waste is released into our water systems and reservoirs and even directly into the sea.

The phrase throw-away society has never been more appropriate, with disposable nappies, plates, plastic cups, bin liners, food containers, sanitary products, designer clothes that are out of fashion and 'need' replacing each year.

Endless advertising ensures a steady stream of customers for all the products which manufacturers tell us we need. None of these are so essential that we could not do away with them and most, if not all, have healthy, natural alternatives that we could use instead.

Make a list of the ways in which you already contribute to this destruction of the earth. Car use, air travel, using chemical based pesticides and chemicals in house-hold products, cosmetics and toiletries which are toxic or have been tested on animals. Be honest and write down every thing you can think of – even energy use in the home, electricity and gas, are produced using natural resources and contribute to climate change through the pollution which is produced in their use and making.

Do some research into the products you use and the environmental impact of your life-style. Find out how you are contributing to the damage of the earth. Some of the chemicals contained in products we put onto our skin are not only damaging to the environment, but to our own health. Are you sure your clothing has not been made in sweatshops? Has your food been over-packaged, treated with chemicals and flown thousands of miles to reach you in perfect condition? Does your gardening include petro-chemical slug-pellets or plant food? Does your soap contain harmful parabens? Write down everything you can think of. How long is your list?

When we talk about Wicca as an earth-based religion, we must not just talk the talk, but must try, as far as we are able, to walk the walk. We are duty bound to celebrate and revere the earth and can choose to reclaim our position as guardians of the earth.

How can we try to sustain and nourish our spirits if our bodies are fed genetically engineered foods and plastered with skin creams that are carcinogenic or hormone disrupting?

Now compile a list of all the things you are currently doing to try and combat the damage and desecration. Buying organic food, using naturally produced cleaning products and recycling glass, paper, metal and plastic are all things you may already do. Do you have energy saving light bulbs and always switch off the tap when you brush your teeth? Have you stopped smoking or started to take a bus to work instead of your car? Write down everything you can think of.

Compare the two lists. The first is likely to be considerably longer than the second. To try and make the changes necessary in the world to improve our chances of combating climate change, pollution and improving our health and environment in general, there are several sources we can turn to for help. Contact the organisations listed at the back of this book and see if they have any resources or ideas that you want to use. Enrich your list of positive actions.

Composting toilets are a natural and safe alternative to flushing and recycles our bodily wastes to use as fertiliser. Using cloth sanitary towels to be washed and re-used is a hygienic way of combating the negative effects that bleached, pesticide containing cotton tampons or towels can have on our sensitive skin. Cloth nappies are far better for babies' skin, surprisingly easy to wash, usually shaped to fit with no complicated folding and come ready with easy to use press-stud or Velcro fastenings.

Several resources have information on how to make your own house-hold and beauty products using simple, cheap and natural ingredients. Try to buy at least one organic item every time you shop and look for fairly traded alternatives to your favourite brands of coffee, tea and clothing. Recycled paper is not difficult to get hold of and you can get great exercise by cycling twice a week instead of spending a minor fortune by driving to a gym.

Other ways to help include supporting local environmental and human or animal rights campaign groups. This does not mean you have to live on a muddy protest site or get arrested. You could give support to environmental actions by way of donations, painting banners, offering legal or medical support to national and local organisations. Plant a tree for every one thousand miles that you drive to soak up your carbon footprint. It would only take a few minutes of your time to write a letter to your MP about local environmental concerns. You might chose to give time and energy to a charity shop once a week or buy second-hand goods for yourself and as gifts for others. Support local trade and reduce your pollution output by walking to the nearby farmer's market instead of driving to the supermarket. See if a Freecycle network is operating in your area. Freecycle is a network of people worldwide who exchange goods for free instead of taking their unwanted items to a tip for incineration or dumping on a land-fill site. One woman's rubbish is another woman's treasure, after all.

Being Wiccan in western society can bring with it the desire to buy the latest book, the best black clothing, the shiniest pentacle or crystal. It can mean going to rituals and Sabbats and celebrating national earth day with an annual litter-pick. It can also mean that we truly try to walk our talk. All of the ideas above are spiritual practices for they are done with the best of intentions for healing and protecting our environment, for ourselves and for each other. Without positive action on the physical level, all our talk of being Pagan or Wiccan is meaningless. Every positive action, no matter how dirty the cans we collect for recycling or how sore our feet after a protest march, can be done with a spiritual awareness of how we are contributing to earth healing. We are one with the earth and protecting it is our duty, our birthright and our ritual.

10

Cycles and Seasons

As Wiccans, we have a major festival roughly every six weeks, with four of those being marked out as the Greater Sabbats. The Greater Sabbats are Imbolc, Beltane, Lammas and Samhain. The Lesser Sabbats are Ostara, Litha, Mabon and Yule. The Lesser four mark the winter and summer solstices and the two equinoxes during spring and autumn.

Also called the fire festivals, the Greater Sabbats have fixed dates whereas the lesser festivals have slightly varying dates, depending on when exactly the solstices and equinoxes fall.

Imbolc
1st February – Greater Sabbat.
Fixed Date.

Also known as Oimelc, meaning very literally 'ewe's milk', or Candlemass, this is the beginning of spring, when lambs are born and the first green shoots come up from the ground. Candles are a major feature of this ritual and we honour the Goddess Bride or Brighid as the maiden, bringer of life and very often, a ritual focus for Imbolc will be to welcome in the Goddess and the returning light. White robes, spring flowers and organic milk are commonly used in the Imbolc ritual, along with as many candles as you can safely manage. We celebrate the new life and returning of the sun after the dark

of winter. We plant the seeds of anything we want to grow over the course of the year – material or otherwise. This is also the time of year traditionally used for initiations into the craft.

The dark Goddess of winter gives way to her maiden counterpart at this time of year and she begins to watch over the new year, bringing us inspiration and new beginnings. The God at this time of year is young also, the Oak King has taken over the throne from the dark Holly King and he will watch over the first half of the year, as he gains strength and confidence, the sun gains strength also. He is son of the Goddess and will become her lover at Beltane.

Ostara
21st March – Lesser Sabbat.
Day of the Equinox varies.

While the date of the actual equinox may be the 20th or 22nd, most Wiccans hold their celebration on the 21st. Ostara, or Eostare, is the festival of eggs, signifying the rebirth and continuance of all things, the Goddess Ostara (corresponding with the female hormone oestrogen) starts to germinate the seeds we have planted and flowers may be in bloom already.

The Goddess and God are not yet lovers but are touting for affection at this time. The sun begins to visibly lighten our evenings and early mornings, baby birds are getting ready to fly and the earth comes alive with the promise of warmth.

Beltane
1st May – Greater Sabbat.
Fixed Date.

Beltane is a fire festival, with bonfires and maypoles to dance around. The maypole is the symbolic phallus of the God, erect and looking for love, the white and red ribbons wound around it in the dancing are the milk and menstrual flow of the Goddess, representing her readiness for love. This is the traditional time for hand-fastings (Wiccan wedding). Many animals start their mating season in May and the sun is making itself clearly known as the God, the Oak King, grows in strength – virile and frisky. He chases after the Goddess, she turns into a deer and runs, he becomes a white stag and finally catches her and they mate with soul-deep love for each other and the Earth. The traditions of the May Queen and the green-wood marriages stem from this story.

Babies conceived at Beltane will be born at the festival of Imbolc, completing the circle and starting it again as they grow bigger and stronger. Beltane morning dew is said to make you beautiful if you wash with it and the faerie folk come out to play in the woodlands on May Eve.

Litha

21st June – Lesser Sabbat.
Day of the Solstice varies.

Litha is the summer solstice. The height of the warmth and bounty in the earth are celebrated in this festival. A time for being outdoors, enjoying warmth and first signs of the coming harvest as the crops begin to grow, fed by the sunlight of the young, strong God. A time for feasting with friends and family, watching the sun set and rise on the longest day of the year. We honour the Goddess and God as bringers of love and happiness, warmth and comfort.

At Litha, the God as the Oak King, is challenged to his place on the throne by his winter-self, the Holly King. The Goddess presides over the fight. As the Oak King is slain and Holly King takes control of the sun, there is only brief mourning of the changing season, for the Oak King's power is not gone yet and there will still be warmth and growing crops for some time yet. The Holly King is the more mature consort of the Goddess as she herself becomes wiser and more nurturing.

Lammas
1st August – Greater Sabbat.
Fixed Date.

Also called Lughnasadh (pronounced loo – na – sah) meaning feast of the God Lugh, the sun king who watches over the corn. Lamas translates literally as 'loaf – mass'. This is when the first fruits of the coming harvest are being seen in the fields and bushes, berries and soft fruits are picked, corn is almost ready to be picked and in old times and new times alike, farmers make ready to bring in the harvest. Tradition dictates that we bake home-made bread to share at the Lammas ritual and mead is the drink of choice.

As for the God and Goddess at this time, she is the mother now, often seen at Lammas as the corn Goddess Ceres, pouring bounty onto the world. The God, in his aspect of the Holly King, represents the darkness to come and brings us darker mornings and evenings, he brings on the night, even though the sun is still strong during daylight hours.

Mabon
21st September – Lesser Sabbat.
Day of Equinox varies.

The autumn equinox is about feasting and parties, the crops have been brought in and this festival is held to give thanks to the Goddess and God for the bounty provided, the bounty of crops and fruit, the bounty of friendships, thanks for all our gifts. Thanks are given to the Goddess especially as she brings forth the seeds – plants or dreams – we asked for at Imbolc. There is a strong and long tradition of saving the very last sheaf of wheat to be cut and making this into a corn dolly, often called a Maiden. The Maiden would hold the spirit of the corn inside it and was taken indoors with care and kept safe and honoured until the spring time planting season began again, at which time the spirit was released so it could enter the new crops as they began to germinate in the earth.

As with the first of May, the autumnal equinox is steeped in history and there are countless traditions, folklore and customs that surround the festival, from the Abbots Bromley horn dance and Morris dancing and Hobby horses to the Wild Hunt. Many of the old traditions either continue in some form or are being revived in small towns and even some larger cities hold annual celebrations on these dates. Even if they are not overtly Pagan in nature today, they have distinct overtones of older customs and the public are welcome to join in the celebrations.

Samhain
31st October – Greater Sabbat.
Fixed Date

Samhain (pronounced 'sow-een') is when we gather in rituals to honour our Beloved Dead. The Holly King has gained in strength and brings with him darkness and bad weather. Our ancestors killed off their weakest animals and dried the meat to last them through the winter. A great feast is held at Samhain as people gather to tell ghost stories, play games and tell fortunes. It is said that the veil between the worlds is thinner at Samhain than any other time of year. We celebrate the lives of those who have passed on, mourn recent losses, share memories and send our thoughts, prayers and messages onwards, asking for our Beloved Dead to come to us if they wish to and are able to.

The Holly King is in his element at Samhain, with dark evenings and early mornings, signs of winter are seen in the natural world and the God is old and dark, a wise man to whom we can turn for guidance through dark times in our lives. The Goddess comes to us as the Crone, the old wise woman who cuts the threads of life. She is the destroyer and many dread her cold hand, but she is not evil, for everything must have an end, even life. For everything the Crone takes away, nature will give something back to fill the void. Death is seen by Pagans and Wiccans not as the end but as a continuance in the cycle of life, with a firm belief in reincarnation.

Yule
21st December – Lesser Sabbat.
Day of the Solstice varies.

The winter solstice is the shortest day and longest night, although the earlier sun rises will not be evident for about another week. The Holly King and the Oak King once again fight, this time the Oak King is victorious and the Holly King gives up his place on the throne and dies, as the winter now begins to die. The Goddess is still the winter Crone, dark, shrouded and cackling; yet even as the bringer of death, she allows the sun God to be reborn, ensuring the Wheel of the Year continues to turn and the summer and happiness return once more.

The Christmas traditions many of us have grown up with do not have to vanish from our lives as we find our way along the Wiccan path. Many of them were Pagan to begin with. Our ancestors would bring a live tree into the house to give the tree spirits somewhere warm to live during winter; Prince Albert reintroduced the practice in 1841, after which time it became common in Britain once more. Holly wreaths were made as a reminder, with their evergreen leaves, that summer will come again. The traditional Yule log, saved from the hearth fire at the solstice, was kept and used to light the next Yule fire, symbolising continual warmth through the depth of winter and the continuity of nature. The tradition of gift giving, originating from the Norse legend of Odin rewarding his followers with gifts, has become a great commercial scandal, with people, especially children, demanding better and bigger gifts each year. Many Pagans choose to give something more worthwhile and environmen-tally sound to our loved ones. Consider giving whale adoption certificates or have a tree planted for someone instead of some mass marketed, over packaged trinket that will probably sit for months unused.

Many standing stone circles and stone cairns are aligned to the sunrise at the winter solstice (some to the midsummer solstice), emphasising the importance of this date to our ancestors. Yule is a time to gather with friends and family for tales by the warming fire, with good food and warm drinks to see us through the dark nights.

As the Wheel of the Year turns again towards spring and Imbolc, we see not completion of a cycle, for a circle has no ending, we see instead the cycle of continuation, emergence and rebirth.

Sabbat Rituals

To create a ritual for any Sabbat or other celebration, it is helpful to follow a set pattern, deviating from it where appropriate and including anything specifically related to the theme of the Sabbat.

Theme – select a theme to run throughout the ritual; harvest, rebirth, honouring the ancestors etc.

Preparation – put everything you will need together on or near your altar. Cleanse yourself and your sacred space. Write a poem to sum up the spirit of the festival or create a simple script to follow if you like something structured.
Cast a circle – invoking the elements and Goddess and God in whatever aspects are suitable to the overall theme.

Action – cast a spell for fertility at Imbolc, act out the Beltane chase of the God and Goddess, honour your beloved dead at Samhain, hold a feast for the Mabon harvest with friends, make love, dance or read poetry. Your own ideas will be far more potent for you than anything you ever see written down.

Cone of Power – the raising and releasing of energy. Even if there is nothing you need energy for, it can still be raised and sent out for general healing of the earth or her people.

Grounding – finish any ritual or spell working with a grounding exercise to anchor you to the physical plane.

Blessing – consecrate food and drink and offer some to the earth as a token of thanks.

Close – give thanks to the Goddess and God and to each element. Close your circle and let any remaining energy drift back to the universal source.

Clean Up – put away all the trappings of ritual; this is especially important when rituals are performed out of doors. Not a scrap of candle wax or hint of litter should be left and after you leave it, the place should be as tidy or tidier than it was to begin with.

The Moon

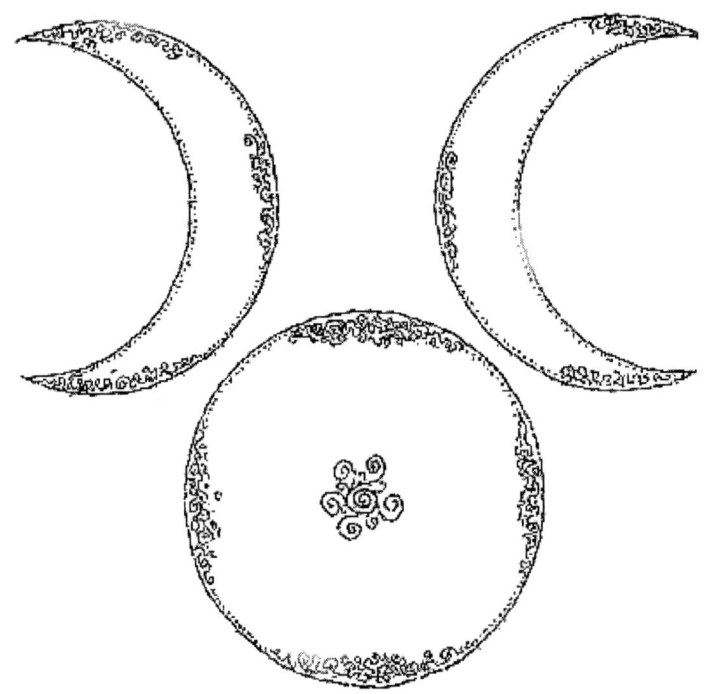

Enchanted am I by this Great Lady,
Reflecting her light upon my face.
All seeing, all knowing, wise and just,
She speaks silently in the night.
Her voice, like silver arrows,
Pierces the heart with love.
By her presence I am caught,
Entrapped with her gaze.
Beautiful moon, she shines so bright
Letting her all-forgiving light
Bless all the creatures of the night.
Tranced, entranced, enchanted
Am I by this Great Lady.

Often referred to as 'she', the moon exerts a powerful influence on the Earth and all of its creatures. It is the force of the moon that dictates the turning of the tides and our own bodies are also influenced by the moon. It is from the moon - Luna - that we get the word lunacy and it has been widely documented that there are more instances of crime, violence, and irrational behaviour when the moon is full. More people are admitted into psychiatric care during the full moon and patients really do become more disturbed and agitated when the moon is full

Women's menstrual cycles are closely linked with the moon and most women will have their periods at the same time of the lunar month, rather than the calendar month. The average 28-day menstrual cycle corresponds with the 28-day lunar cycle and babies are more accurately gestated for ten lunar months, rather than nine of man's calendar. There are even documented court cases of women who commit crimes during their menses actually having reduced sentences as menstruation has been seen as mitigating circumstances.

As you follow the cycle of the moon over the course of several months, try to keep track of your moods and emotions and, if you are a woman, your menses. Compare your moods to the magical associations of each moon phase and see if they correspond with each other.

Moon Phases and Associations
New & Waxing Moon – visible in the sky after a period of darkness as a crescent pointing to the left. This phase of the moon is for new projects, fertility, new beginnings and increase. Youth, love, birth and intuition are also the province of the new moon. The Goddess is seen as the youthful virgin, the Maiden, at the new and waxing moon. She is fertile yet pure and innocent, playful and enticing. The Maiden is the fate who weaves the thread of life.

Full Moon – the moon is full when seen as a complete globe in the sky. The full moon can be used for any kind of magic as the moon is at its most powerful at this time. The full moon represents mothering, bringing things to fruition, the materialisation of dreams and desires, success, the wholeness and unity of all things. Traditionally, it is the full moon that is most often associated with witchcraft. The Goddess is thought of as the Mother during the full moon, heavy with pregnancy or holding a child. The Mother is the caring, nurturing lover; protective and bold. The Mother is the one who measures the thread of life.

Waning and Dark Moon – the waning moon is seen as a crescent pointing to the right, like the letter 'C'. The dark moon is said to be the three days when the moon can no longer be seen in the sky at all. Used for getting rid of things, breaking harmful habits, binding spells and banishing or releasing things. This is the time when grief and death can be honoured. The dark moon is also the time when our ancestors would have carried out hexes and curses. The Goddess in her Crone aspect makes herself known at the dark and waning moon. The Crone can be sinister, dark and brooding, she is the bringer of death. The Crone is often feared but without death there would be no life. She is the secret keeper and wise old woman. The Crone is the one who cuts the thread of life.

Blue Moon - When a Full Moon occurs twice in one month, the second full moon is a blue moon. This is an excellent time to set new goals for yourself; it is said that whatever you wish for at this time will come true. Be careful what you wish for – it may well come to pass!

Lunar Eclipse – The Lunar Eclipse represents the union of both male and female energies of the Sun and Moon, any type of magic worked or energy sent out during a lunar eclipse will be greatly amplified. An eclipsing moon is seen to go through every phase and this is very powerful as it brings us the beginning, middle and the end result of whatever we ask for.

Moon Magic

Find a safe place outdoors where you will not be disturbed on a cloudless night and look up at the moon.

Raise your arms up high and breathe deeply, with each breath visualise the moon energy coming into the energy centres of your palms.

Draw the moonlight into your hands and place your hands on each of your chakra points in turn. Feel the power and light of the moon shining down, let it wash over you. Let your mind be open to any visions or images or thoughts that come to you. Do this through several moon cycles and phases, compare the differing energy of each phase.

Other ways to use the moon energy may come to you intuitively or you can adapt the examples given below.

Place a glass of water on your windowsill overnight so that it can soak up the full moon light and drink it the following morning. Feel yourself being filled with the silvery loving light of the mother moon.

Crystals can be left on a window ledge to be charged with moon energy and used for healing or spells.

Cast a circle and invoke the elements. Call down the Moon Goddess, ask her to fill you with moon energy and feel yourself being empowered, confident and capable.

> *Triple Goddess of the Moon, I call you into my circle. May I be blessed with clear thoughts, intuition and creativity.*

If you have something particular on your mind, sit quietly and ask the Goddess for guidance – open yourself to the probability of visions and images and random thoughts.

The full moon is a good time to carry out divination so this is an appropriate time for getting out your rune stones or tarot cards. If you are not adept at these forms of divination, you could try making your own set of personalised fortune stones and spread them out at the full moon ritual.

Any moon phase can be used for healing magic with the new and waxing moon bringing healing and the waning or dark moon to banish illness and the full moon representing the fullness of normal health.

Sing a song, play a tune or hum a melody and dance for the moon. Read a poem for the moon and give your thanks for Her presence in your life.

Close your circle in the normal way and do some form of grounding exercise, even stamping your feet and clapping your hands can work as a way of grounding. Pay particular attention to your dreams after any moon celebration, as the moon energy can enhance your intuition and bring you powerful insights into your life and the situations and people around you.

11

The Haberdashery for Spells and Ritual

The elements work in harmony together; without water and sunlight, plants (earth) would die, without air and matter, fire could not exist. We must then use the elements in conjunction with each other when we want to do spell casting.

It is vital to magic and rituals that our will power and intuition are not overshadowed by the trappings and tools that some of us use. None of these things are needed and two examples are already given for Spirit, thought-form and connection, which can be done very successfully with nothing more than your own will power and determination to make it work. Tools are useful as an aid to concentration and to focus our intention into something practical that we can 'do'.

Intuition is our greatest ally in Wicca and should never be ignored or pushed aside just because a certain spell book says we need three peacock feathers and pinch of graveyard dust. If you have a pigeon feather and soil from your back yard, there is no reason why these will not serve just as well, providing the symbolism is relevant to your desire. It should be obvious by now that all magic is based on the principle of focused intention and has little to do with tools or material objects.

It is clear then, that to create a successful spell we need to think carefully about what actions we can do to aid our concentration on the issue.

Air is the beginning, the intellectual thought behind the spell, fire is the energy and desire we use to get it under way, water represents the emotions involved and is the tide that carries us to earth – the physical action we need to carry out to manifest our goals. Spirit is the intention and energy we raise and focus on to achieve the goal and the Goddess and God act as our conscience and guide us to making the right decisions or actions.

Having said this, it can be useful to have symbolic representations to help us focus and channel our energy. Some general objects that can be used for spell casting are listed here for your convenience, although they are only ideas to use as a guideline.

Colours are used a lot in spell casting and there can be conflicting opinions about what each colour means. Go with your instincts and use whichever colour seems to suit your purpose or seems pleasing.

> Red indicates fire, love, fertility, passion and anger.
>
> Blue represents the elements of water and air, interviews, exams, learning, communication and serenity.
>
> Yellow is used for travel, career, communication and wealth.
>
> Brown is for earth, practical and material matters, home, animals and children.

Pink is for friendship, healing and love.

Green is earth, money, growth and careers.

Orange is for general well being, happiness and prosperity.

Purple promotes the development of spirituality, psychic ability, wisdom and divination.

White is used for purity, truth, honesty, beginnings and fertility, cleansing and peace.

Black is for the release of guilt and anger, banishing and binding magic.

Gold represents the sun, money, material wealth and life changes.

Silver is associated with the moon, dreams, prophecy and the inner self.

Crystals are powerful allies at their most basic level but when cleansed, consecrated and charged with universal energy can provide us with a stream of specific energy for months at a stretch with little or no further attention. Wear a crystal ring or pendant to keep the energy with you constantly, use for special occasions or add to a talisman pouch.

Amber is a cure-all, bestowing general happiness, contentment and healing, it is a happy stone.

Amethyst is a spiritual crystal, giving intuition and helping to develop psychic senses.

Moonstone is clearly related to the moon's energy and is good for women with painful or irregular menstrual cycles and is also useful as an aid to intuitive knowledge and healing.

Rose Quartz is a wonderful healer and also represents love, including platonic love, rose quartz can help almost any situation.

Blue Lace Agate is good for communication issues, especially within close relationships.

Citrine is good for ensuring we are happy with our levels of wealth.

Cords and ribbons can be used to weave dream catchers or woven to wear as a bracelet or charm. Find some ribbons or cords in appropriate colours to wear around your wrist or keep under your bed. Tie in some feathers or charms or use ribbons to sew up a talisman pouch.

Candles are related to the fire element and can be found in a wide range of colours. They can be anointed with essential oils and etched with relevant words or symbols to bring about the spell. If a candle is very large and you have little time spare for the ritual, push several needles all the way through the candle at regular intervals and each time the flame burns to the needle mark, snuff out the flame. As not all of the candle's energy has been burned out, it can be relit at a later stage when you have time to let it burn down further, without letting the energy of the spell dissipate.

Feathers from particular birds or bird images might be appropriate for some spells. Birds of prey are known for their keen eyesight and help you see a situation the way it really is, cuckoos are a sign of spring and so you might want to draw on that energy to bring you new life and energy.

Draw or write on paper which can be burned to transform something, buried to let it grow or immersed in water to dissipate negative energy. Paper can be used to write down positive affirmations and kept as a talisman hidden under your pillow or in the depths of a hand-bag. Use coloured paper and pens to enhance the symbolism.

Talismans are personalised charms that can be carried around with you to remind you of your pledge or spell and so add energy to the idea of it coming to you. Take some natural fabric in a suitable colour and place seashells, feathers, coins, pebbles, paper or any other items that represent your spell in the middle. Consecrate any ingredients and sew it up. Charge the finished talisman pouch and keep it with you at all times.

Balloons can be blown up with our anger and then bashed and popped to release it. They can also be filled with helium and carry our desires for resolving communication difficulties into the air.

Mirrors and silver are both reflective and can be used to ward off negative energy and harm. Mirrors are good for self-development work, looking at our reflection as we say our positive affirmations can reinforce the message and encourage us to change the way we view ourselves if we have a poor self-image.

Coins can be useful as a way of attracting more wealth to us; it is said that like attracts like, after all. Try putting coins into a gold or orange bag with sigils like the pound sign or the words money, prosperity on a piece of paper. Add a piece of amber to ensure that you will still be happy once you get the wealth you require.

Symbols of any kind can be used in our spell castings. The triple moon symbol, a full circle with a crescent on either side, can add the power of the moon to a spell, especially if left in view of the moon overnight or longer. A pink heart represents love, a horseshoe can bring good luck and a picture of a wise old owl would help with decision making and so on.

12

Spells for Peace and Happiness

All of these spells are included as ideas which you may follow to the letter or, preferably, adapt and personalise to make the results work better for you.

It is assumed that you will prepare yourself and your working area and cast a circle before any spell working and close the sacred space afterwards. Remember to consecrate and, if appropriate, charge any tools or materials you use and keep the intention of the spell positive throughout.

With all of the spells suggested below and any that you invent yourself, it would be beneficial to add the following words or something very like them to complete and seal the spell.

> *Ancient Goddess, hear my call,*
> *Let this spell work for the good of all.*

Or,

> *By the Power of the Goddess and God,*
> *All are wished well with this benevolent spell.*

Amber Good Luck Charm

Take a small piece of amber and go out into strong sunlight. Put the amber onto a piece of copper or gold to enhance the power of the sun and repeat the chant three times.

> *Sun God, Sky God I ask thee*
> *Bring hope and happiness now to me.*
> *Charge this crystal with your power*
> *Make it so within the hour.*

Leave the amber to soak up the sunlight for one hour, move it back in the sun if a shadow threatens to fall on the crystal. Put it in under your pillow at night and keep it with you during the day.

Rose Quartz Healing Spell

Our spiritual and physical well being are interconnected and it is impossible to balance the two unless we work on both levels. If you are working magic to heal a person, it is equally important that they see a doctor who can work with you on the physical level to heal them. If they have not been to a doctor, encourage them to do so at the earliest opportunity.

Obtain a bottle of rose water and put a piece of rose quartz crystal in it. Leave it to charge for three nights during the waxing moon, asking the Moon Goddess to charge it with healing energy every day.

Remove the rose quartz and discard the water. Put the crystal in a sunny spot for three days and ask the Sun God to charge it with powerful healing energy every day.

In sacred space, put the crystal on your altar and bless it with each element. Raise a cone of power and channel all of the energy raised into the crystal. Attach it to a chain or put into a small charm bag to be worn by the person who needs the healing.

Yarrow Moon Spell

For those times of the month, ladies, when the aches and pains of pre-menstrual tension strike with a vengeance, gather a some yarrow leaves and flowers. Yarrow is commonly found on grass verges, scrublands and meadows; it is a small white to pinkish flower with tiny petals and feathery green leaves; use a good botanical guide to find the right plant and rinse it under the tap before use. Yarrow is good at easing or curing the symptoms of menstruation and can even lessen the blood-flow.

Lay the yarrow on the altar with some lavender essential oil and ask for the Goddess in her Mother aspect to bless the plant. Light a red candle, anointed with the lavender oil. Ask the Mother Goddess to provide you with comfort and ease and let the fire element provide soothing warmth, feel it coming into you through your hands and transfer it to each of your chakras. Massage some of the lavender oil into your abdomen to help ease any cramping pains and make an infusion of yarrow tea by pouring just-boiled water over it. When cool enough, strain and drink the tea twice a day, until your symptoms are relieved. This can be repeated every month if necessary.

Protection Charm

To protect your lover while you are apart, take a white candle and engrave it with the words protection, security, guardian and any other words that come to you.

Anoint the candle with rose oil (roses have thorns which protect the delicate flowers and the rose is also associated with love).

Push several rose thorns into the candle itself as a symbol of protection.

Write on a piece of white paper the words love, protection and security. Follow this with a rough sketch or photograph of your loved one and their name.

Light the candle and burn the paper. As it turns to ash, imagine your lover being surrounded by a brilliant white light, forming a solid shell around them, which will protect them while you are apart.

Animal Protector

To protect you while you are in dangerous situations, walking home late at night for example, carry out a ritual to develop a thought-form, as you did for working with spirit in chapter eight. Build up a strong image of the animal you feel would protect you best in your particular situation; a large and fierce-looking dog trotting by your side, or a horse to transport you home safely. Ask the animal to stay with you and protect you as you travel.

This thought-form could become a regular companion or guardian if you use it frequently and will gain potency the more you call on it for assistance. Remember to thank the animal-form when it has done its job for you. If you think you will want to call on its help in future, tell it so and the next time you want to use it, call on its energy and add more to it to bring it to 'life' again.

Serenity

Sometimes it is hard to feel fully alive in our western world, with all the things that go on around us and that we are involved in. Take time out of your schedule to follow this exercise and bring serenity.

Stand tall and ground yourself, feel the energy coming through the floor, up through your body. Hold your arms up above your head and pull energy with deep breaths into you from above. Once you have a flow of energy from above and below, reach up and feel yourself drifting upwards with the energy.

Imagine you are going above the roof or over the tree canopy, up into the sky. Go further up and further still, reach the outer limits of the sky and see yourself entering space. Look at the stars and head towards one of them. Hold your hands out and pick up a star in each hand, feeling it tingle on your skin with pulsing, gentle light. This light has never been to earth, never been busy or stressed out. Focus on coming down to earth again, bringing the star's light with you, entering the atmosphere again and coming back down slowly into your body. Bring the light into your aura and feel it mixing with your own energy, adding a calming and serene influence to your life.

The Invisible Ingredient

One simple spell that can be used for any occasion and will bring a smile to you every time you use it is the invisible cooking ingredient.

Find an empty jar or pot with a lid and every time you cook something, take it out and dip your fingers deep inside, as though taking out some special, sacred ingredient.

The invisible ingredient you are putting into your food is love. Cook with love for those you are feeding, even if you do not feel loving towards them at the time. When you cook with the intention of creating the food with love for those who will eat it, you will find your cooking and eating experience is transformed into an act of beauty.

Put this special magic into all your recipes and smile, with love, as you serve up the food and see how many people take second helpings.

Fertility

It is said that any woman who wishes to become pregnant cannot fail in her task if she makes love on the eye of the white chalk horse of Uffington or the tip of the phallus of the Cerne Abbas giant. In fact, as any visitor to Cerne Abbas will be able to verify, the giant is set into a steep hillside and the tip of the penis has been worn over time into a shallow dip, clear evidence that lovers still carry out the old tradition!

To aid fertility, it helps if a woman is able to detect her most fertile days each month and accurately predict them. Following your menstrual cycle will give you a good indication of this over several months. Ovulation usually occurs roughly halfway between menstrual bleeds and is often accompanied by tender breasts, slight cramping pains and a higher than usual desire to make love and this is the best time to try for a baby.

Make a talisman pouch from natural white cloth and put images of babies and baby related paraphernalia inside, together with a picture of you and your partner. Add some rose petals, love hearts and any other symbols of love and parenthood that seem appropriate. Keep this under your mattress until you have safely had your baby.

Go into a journey and ask your Guide to help you find a safe place where you can meet with the Goddess. Ask the Triple Goddess of the moon to appear to you in all three guises. Talk with her Maiden aspect, ask her to bless you with the new life of a child inside you, a new dawn for you as you start the journey of pregnancy. Ask the Mother aspect to share motherhood with you, to give you the loving and nurturing experience of motherhood. Ask the Crone aspect of the Goddess to bless you with an ending to your state of childless life, ask her to take away anything which is stopping you from conceiving a child.

Give thanks to the Goddess and close your sacred space as you normally would.

Light a white or silver candle to represent the child you long for, carve it with words like pregnancy, baby, love, family. Light the candle every time you make love.

Restore Harmony

To ease tension between you and your partner, work colleagues, friends or children, weave some yellow or pale blue ribbons in with some feathers and charge them. Now wind it around the base of a yellow or pale blue candle and ask the element of air to help clear the air between you. Have another, larger feather ready to sweep around yourself to release tension and eliminate stress in your own aura and mentally carry out the same exercise around the other person's aura too if they are willing to take part in the ritual, otherwise just visualise that they are being cleansed of any bad feelings towards you.

Sprinkle water on the ribbons and feathers, asking the element of water to bring balance back into the relationship. Take the ribbons with you (hidden in your bag or pocket if necessary) next time you see the person or people involved and breathe in a deliberate aura of serenity before you speak. You can also protect yourself with a golden aura protection spell before you meet them, especially if you want to address the underlying issues between you.

New Job

If you are having problems with finding a job, write a description of the job you would most like to have, one that fits in with all your expectations concerning location, time, salary, colleagues and bosses and the actual nature of the work.

Read this out in the circle and ask the Goddess and God to bring the job to you. Build up a clear picture of how you will look, walk, talk and feel once you have the job you are looking for. Imagine what your colleagues will be like, the type of building you work in, the sort of things you are doing. See the wage slip (be realistic) and yourself smiling as you receive it. The more you add to this mental image, the more effective it will be.

Raise a cone of power and hold your thoughts and images clearly throughout. Let the energy pour down on you and your ideal job description and soak it all up until you are full, then ground yourself.

Remember to look in all the places and papers you would normally turn to for job advertisements and keep your thoughts on having a secure job already, rather than finding one soon – keep magic in the present, if you project thoughts about getting a job tomorrow, you will soon find that tomorrow is unattainable. (This is a rule worth following for all your spells).

Wealth

There are many ways to be rich. You can be rich in material terms, good house, nice car, lots of money. But wouldn't you prefer to be rich in terms of friendship, comfort, stability and family?

Most people are not convinced that money won't bring happiness and of course, we all need to have money to pay the bills. For times when happy friendships and quality times with family are not providing a healthy bank balance, carry out the following spell on a Sunday, at noon, on a sunny day.

Put some coins on a gold coloured or orange plate or bowl and take it outside. Sit in the sun and think of what you need financially. Have a realistic goal in mind.

Look up to the sky and call upon the horned God, the father of all, to help you. Ask him for the money you need and tell him what you need it for.

Leave the money outside in a safe, preferably sunny, place and bring it in again as the sun begins to go down or sooner if it rains.

Put the money safely away in a pot or jar and when you get your requested financial help, give this money away to charity as a way of thank you to the God for helping you out in times of need.

Preparing for Action

We have touched on the subject of caring for Mother Earth in both spiritual and practical ways. This might involve taking part in an organised march or demonstration as part of a larger group and while these actions hope to have some impact on the situations we are trying to change, it can be very daunting and nerve-wracking for those taking part.

Before you embark on any demonstration, march or protest, take five or ten minutes sitting or standing still, either with your companions or alone.

Be silent. Acknowledge the power of both God and Goddess deep within yourself. Open a thread of running energy from above and below, as in the tree of life exercise from chapter three. Make a deep connection with the energy of nature and lift your hands to the sky. Ask the Old Ones, aloud or silently, to give you the strength and empowerment you need to carry through with your actions. Ask for protection and peace as you carry out the march or demonstration.

Breathe in deeply a few times, with each breath acknowledge that you are strong and powerful, you are calm and confident.

Let the gentle, natural energy stay with you as you go off with your fellow protestors and keep that thread of running energy in mind that you may draw upon it if you start to feel anxious or drained.

Rather than being a spell in the usual sense of the word, this is the sort of spiritual work that you can undertake for any cause. As you progress through the Craft your connection with the elements will deepen and this sort of work will become more and more beneficial to your daily life.

Activist Support Ritual

For when environmental actions are going on in your area but you don't want to take a physical part in it yourself, there are many things you can do to support the cause.

Cast a circle and invoke as normal, have some representation present of what the action is about, a leaflet about the action, a sticker or badge for instance.

Light a candle on top of or next to this item and imagine all of the protestors being surrounded by the protective light of the candle. Visualise the circle of light glowing around each person involved in the action and see them protected.

Make an appeal to the God and Goddess that these people be honoured, treated with respect by the police or by-standers and have a peaceful demonstration.

Keep the visualisation up for as long as you can manage it and raise a cone of power, sending the energy to the protestors. Ask for them to achieve their goals.

After you have closed the circle, telephone or visit any activists you know who were involved and see if they need anything you can offer; legal support, healing, a shoulder to lean on, someone to bring them hot food if the action is ongoing.

Banishing and Binding Spells*
Binding magic is done to literally bind someone from doing harm. Should you ever find yourself being threatened or harassed, binding can help if you know the identity of your enemy. If you are suffering from general ill-luck or discord in your life with no clear reason, banishing can get rid of a streak of bad luck and help take away any negative energy directed at you even if you don't know the cause.

Stop You Charm
To stop someone who is deliberately trying to harm you, either physically or mentally, the first thing you can do on a practical level is to inform the police. Back this up with the following spell, which should only be done if there is a very real risk of actual harm, due to the intense nature of what you are doing on the astral level. It should be made absolutely clear that this spell is not about vengeance or ill-wishing, but about the person's own karma returning to them. Under no circumstances would it be morally right or ethical to strike back with anger or violence and you should work on healing and controlling your own anger before deciding to bind anyone. It is not a way of harming a person, rather it can ensure they have no power over you and will leave you alone, for their own well being as well as yours.

Take a photograph or draw a picture of the person who wishes you ill and wrap it up tightly with a length of black cotton or ribbon. On a separate piece of paper, write their name, followed by these words (or similar).

I bind you from doing me harm, you have no power over me.
For as long as you hurt me, you shall have no peace.
You will suffer until you leave me alone.
You bring this about by causing me pain, it is of your own devising.
I bind you, I command you, I stop you.
You are bound from doing me harm.

Now wrap this paper around the picture and bind it again with black thread, stating that this person will have no peace until they decide to leave you alone.

Place these bound papers in some black material and secure it three times with black thread or ribbon. Put in a jar or other lidded container and leave it in there until such a time as the malevolence comes to an end. Once this has worked, you must then undo all the bindings and tell the person's image they are free of the bond as you untie the knots and open out the papers. Bury these with the intention of all the energy and negativity surrounding the person and the circumstances being returned to the earth to be reused in a positive way.

Cast Out Evil Spell

Banishing magic is only done to get rid of things we don't like or want in our lives. If you are being plagued by a run of bad luck or a string of illnesses when you are usually fit and healthy, the best way of banishing it is to reflect it away from you.

Take a look around your home and find some object or photograph that represents a happy time in your life, something that makes you feel warm and cosy inside.

Wrap it up in cotton wool and put on your altar inside a circle of white candles. Light the candles one by one, each time say the following words.

Love, trust and harmony,
Happiness, joy and peace.
With all these things in my heart
I cast any evil out.

Picture yourself healthy and content, with the run of illness or disasters ended and bright new things coming to take their place. Let the candles burn down as you project a sphere of white light all around you. Use you aura and chakras to bring energy around you now and push it into place with your hands to create a white, shining barrier of light to keep you safe and stop bad luck getting through.

Repeat the procedure every day until the bad influences are gone from your life.

Mirrors or highly polished metal can be used as a negativity reflector. Put them inside your windows, facing out to reflect away harm and bad luck. Consecrated in the circle and charged with energy raised in a cone of power will make them even more effective.

Put a bag of rusty nails, pins, thorns or other sharp objects under your doorstep, buried if possible, to repel any unwanted visitors. Again, this should be charged with the intention of not harming anyone, merely turning them away if they are bringing you bad luck.

*It cannot be stressed enough that in cases where actual or attempted harm is threatened, the police should be informed at the earliest opportunity.

Further Information

The Pagan Federation provides information on all Pagan paths, offering support and advice to all Pagans. They produce Pagan Dawn magazine and organise Pagan conferences countrywide. They are a non-profit making organisation.
The Pagan Federation,
BM Box 7097,
London WC1N 3XX,
England
www.paganfed.org

British Reclaiming is a network of people coming together for ritual and spirituality with an environmental focus.
Susan Farley
01267 281414
www.reclaim.demon.co.uk

The British Druid Order provides support and information on Druidry.
BDO
PO Box 635
Halifax
HX2 6WX
www.druidorder.demon.co.uk

Children of Artemis provide a similar service to the Pagan Federation and organise the annual 'Witchfest' convention.
Children of Artemis
BM Artemis,
London,
WC1N 3XX
www.witchcraft.org

Based in the USA, **The Witches Voice** provides a very good website with useful information and a lively discussion forum.
The Witches' Voice Inc.,
P.O. Box 4924,
Clearwater,
Florida
33758-4924
U.S.A.
www.witchvox.com

Greenpeace are one of the leading environmental NGO's, with active local and national groups.
Greenpeace
Canonbury Villas,
London,
N1 2PN
www.greenpeace.org.uk

WEN provides information on local and national campaigns concerning women, environment and health.
Women's Environmental Network
PO Box 30626
London
E1 1TZ
www.wen.org.uk

Friends of the Earth campaign on various environmental issues and have local and national groups for actions and networking.
Friends of the Earth
26-28 Underwood Street
LONDON
N1 7JQ
www.foe.co.uk

The Vegetarian Society provides resources and educational information on becoming and staying vegetarian.
The Vegetarian Society of the United Kingdom
Parkdale,
Dunham Road,
Altrincham,
Cheshire,
WA14 4QG
www.vegsoc.org

Oxfam Unwrapped provide unusual, environmentally friendly gifts which benefit people in need.
Oxfam Unwrapped
274 Banbury Rd,
Oxford
OX2 7DZ
www.oxfamunwrapped.com

FREE DETAILED CATALOGUE

Capall Bann is owned and run by people actively involved in many of the areas in which we publish. A detailed illustrated catalogue is available on request, SAE or International Postal Coupon appreciated. **Titles can be ordered direct from Capall Bann, post free in the UK** (cheque or PO with order) or from good bookshops and specialist outlets.

A Breath Behind Time, Terri Hector
A Soul is Born by Eleyna Williamson
Angels and Goddesses - Celtic Christianity & Paganism, M. Howard
The Art of Conversation With the Genius Loci, Barry Patterson
Arthur - The Legend Unveiled, C Johnson & E Lung
Astrology The Inner Eye - A Guide in Everyday Language, E Smith
Auguries and Omens - The Magical Lore of Birds, Yvonne Aburrow
Asyniur - Womens Mysteries in the Northern Tradition, S McGrath
Beginnings - Geomancy, Builder's Rites & Electional Astrology in the European Tradition, Nigel Pennick
Between Earth and Sky, Julia Day
Book of the Veil, Peter Paddon
The Book of Seidr, Runic John
Caer Sidhe - Celtic Astrology and Astronomy, Michael Bayley
Call of the Horned Piper, Nigel Jackson
Can't Sleep, Won't Sleep, Linda Louisa Dell
Carnival of the Animals, Gregor Lamb
Cat's Company, Ann Walker
Celtic Faery Shamanism, Catrin James
Celtic Faery Shamanism - The Wisdom of the Otherworld, Catrin James
Celtic Lore & Druidic Ritual, Rhiannon Ryall
Celtic Sacrifice - Pre Christian Ritual & Religion, Marion Pearce
Celtic Saints and the Glastonbury Zodiac, Mary Caine
Circle and the Square, Jack Gale
Come Back To Life, Jenny Smedley
Compleat Vampyre - The Vampyre Shaman, Nigel Jackson
Creating Form From the Mist - The Wisdom of Women in Celtic Myth and Culture, Lynne Sinclair-Wood
Crystal Clear - A Guide to Quartz Crystal, Jennifer Dent
Crystal Doorways, Simon & Sue Lilly
Crossing the Borderlines - Guising, Masking & Ritual Animal Disguise in the European Tradition, Nigel Pennick
Dragons of the West, Nigel Pennick

Earth Dance - A Year of Pagan Rituals, Jan Brodie
Earth Harmony - Places of Power, Holiness & Healing, Nigel Pennick
Earth Magic, Margaret McArthur
Egyptian Animals - Guardians & Gateways of the Gods, Akkadia Ford
Eildon Tree (The) Romany Language & Lore, Michael Hoadley
Enchanted Forest - The Magical Lore of Trees, Yvonne Aburrow
Eternal Priestess, Sage Weston
Eternally Yours Faithfully, Roy Radford & Evelyn Gregory
Everything You Always Wanted To Know About Your Body, But So Far Nobody's Been Able To Tell You, Chris Thomas & D Baker
Experiencing the Green Man, Rob Hardy & Teresa Moorey
Face of the Deep - Healing Body & Soul, Penny Allen
Fairies and Nature Spirits, Teresa Moorey
Fairies in the Irish Tradition, Molly Gowen
Familiars - Animal Powers of Britain, Anna Franklin
Flower Wisdom, Katherine Kear
Fool's First Steps, (The) Chris Thomas
Forest Paths - Tree Divination, Brian Harrison, Ill. S. Rouse
From Past to Future Life, Dr Roger Webber
From Stagecraft To Witchcraft, , Patricia Crowther
Gardening For Wildlife Ron Wilson
God Year, The, Nigel Pennick & Helen Field
Goddess on the Cross, Dr George Young
Goddess Year, The, Nigel Pennick & Helen Field
Goddesses, Guardians & Groves, Jack Gale
Handbook For Pagan Healers, Liz Joan
Handbook of Fairies, Ronan Coghlan
Healing Book, The, Chris Thomas and Diane Baker
Healing Homes, Jennifer Dent
Healing Journeys, Paul Williamson
Healing Stones, Sue Philips
Herb Craft - Shamanic & Ritual Use of Herbs, Lavender & Franklin
Hidden Heritage - Exploring Ancient Essex, Terry Johnson
Hub of the Wheel, Skytoucher
In and Out the Windows, Dilys Gator
In Search of Herne the Hunter, Eric Fitch
In Search of the Green Man, Peter Hill
Inner Celtia, Alan Richardson & David Annwn
Inner Mysteries of the Goths, Nigel Pennick
Inner Space Workbook - Develop Through Tarot, Cat Summers & Julian Vayne
In Search of Pagan Gods, Teresa Moorey
Intuitive Journey, Ann Walker Isis - African Queen, Akkadia Ford
Journey Home, The, Chris Thomas
Kecks, Keddles & Kesh - Celtic Lang & The Cog Almanac, Bayley
Language of the Psycards, Berenice
Legend of Robin Hood, The, Richard Rutherford-Moore

Lid Off the Cauldron, Patricia Crowther
Light From the Shadows - Modern Traditional Witchcraft, Gwyn
Living Tarot, Ann Walker
Lore of the Sacred Horse, Marion Davies
Lost Lands & Sunken Cities (2nd ed.), Nigel Pennick
The Magic and Mystery of Trees, Teresa Moorey
Magic For the Next 1,000 Years, Jack Gale
Magic of Herbs - A Complete Home Herbal, Rhiannon Ryall
Magical Guardians - Exploring the Spirit and Nature of Trees, Philip Heselton
Magical History of the Horse, Janet Farrar & Virginia Russell
Magical Lore of Animals, Yvonne Aburrow
Magical Lore of Cats, Marion Davies
Magical Lore of Herbs, Marion Davies
Magick Without Peers, Ariadne Rainbird & David Rankine
Masks of Misrule - Horned God & His Cult in Europe, Nigel Jackson
Medicine For The Coming Age, Lisa Sand MD
Medium Rare - Reminiscences of a Clairvoyant, Muriel Renard
Menopausal Woman on the Run, Jaki da Costa
Mind Massage - 60 Creative Visualisations, Marlene Maundrill
Mirrors of Magic - Evoking the Spirit of the Dewponds, P Heselton
The Moon and You, Teresa Moorey
Moon Mysteries, Jan Brodie
Mysteries of the Runes, Michael Howard
Mystic Life of Animals, Ann Walker
New Celtic Oracle The, Nigel Pennick & Nigel Jackson
Oracle of Geomancy, Nigel Pennick
Pagan Feasts - Seasonal Food for the 8 Festivals, Franklin & Phillips
Patchwork of Magic - Living in a Pagan World, Julia Day
Pathworking - A Practical Book of Guided Meditations, Pete Jennings
Personal Power, Anna Franklin
Pickingill Papers - The Origins of Gardnerian Wicca, Bill Liddell
Pillars of Tubal Cain, Nigel Jackson
Places of Pilgrimage and Healing, Adrian Cooper
Planet Earth - The Universe's Experiment, Chris Thomas
Practical Divining, Richard Foord
Practical Meditation, Steve Hounsome
Practical Spirituality, Steve Hounsome
Psychic Self Defence - Real Solutions, Jan Brodie
Real Fairies, David Tame
Reality - How It Works & Why It Mostly Doesn't, Rik Dent
Romany Tapestry, Michael Houghton
Runic Astrology, Nigel Pennick
Sacred Animals, Gordon MacLellan
Sacred Celtic Animals, Marion Davies, Ill. Simon Rouse
Sacred Dorset - On the Path of the Dragon, Peter Knight
Sacred Grove - The Mysteries of the Forest, Yvonne Aburrow

Sacred Geometry, Nigel Pennick
Sacred Nature, Ancient Wisdom & Modern Meanings, A Cooper
Sacred Ring - Pagan Origins of British Folk Festivals, M. Howard
Season of Sorcery - On Becoming a Wisewoman, Poppy Palin
Seasonal Magic - Diary of a Village Witch, Paddy Slade
Secret Places of the Goddess, Philip Heselton
Secret Signs & Sigils, Nigel Pennick
The Secrets of East Anglian Magic, Nigel Pennick
A Seeker's Guide To Past Lives, Paul Williamson
Seeking Pagan Gods, Teresa Moorey
A Seer's Guide To Crystal Divination, Gale Halloran
Self Enlightenment, Mayan O'Brien
Spirits of the Air, Jaq D Hawkins
Spirits of the Water, Jaq D Hawkins
Spirits of the Fire, Jaq D Hawkins
Spirits of the Aether, Jaq D Hawkins
Spirits of the Earth, Jaq D Hawkins
Stony Gaze, Investigating Celtic Heads John Billingsley
Stumbling Through the Undergrowth, Mark Kirwan-Heyhoe
Subterranean Kingdom, The, revised 2nd ed, Nigel Pennick
Symbols of Ancient Gods, Rhiannon Ryall
Talking to the Earth, Gordon MacLellan
Talking With Nature, Julie Hood
Taming the Wolf - Full Moon Meditations, Steve Hounsome
Teachings of the Wisewomen, Rhiannon Ryall
The Other Kingdoms Speak, Helena Hawley
Transformation of Housework, Ben Bushill
Tree: Essence of Healing, Simon & Sue Lilly
Tree: Essence, Spirit & Teacher, Simon & Sue Lilly
Tree Seer, Simon & Sue Lilly
Through the Veil, Peter Paddon
Torch and the Spear, Patrick Regan
Understanding Chaos Magic, Jaq D Hawkins
Understanding Past Lives, Dilys Gater
Understanding Second Sight, Dilys Gater
Understanding Spirit Guides, Dilys Gater
Understanding Star Children, Dilys Gater
The Urban Shaman, Dilys Gater
Vortex - The End of History, Mary Russell
Warp and Weft - In Search of the I-Ching, William de Fancourt
Warriors at the Edge of Time, Jan Fry
Water Witches, Tony Steele
Way of the Magus, Michael Howard
Weaving a Web of Magic, Rhiannon Ryall
West Country Wicca, Rhiannon Ryall
What's Your Poison? vol 1, Tina Tarrant

Wheel of the Year, Teresa Moorey & Jane Brideson
Wildwitch - The Craft of the Natural Psychic, Poppy Palin
Wildwood King , Philip Kane
A Wisewoman's Book of Tea Leaf Reading, Pat Barki
The Witching Path, Moira Stirland
The Witch's Kitchen, Val Thomas
The Witches' Heart, Eileen Smith
Witches of Oz, Matthew & Julia Philips
Wondrous Land - The Faery Faith of Ireland by Dr Kay Mullin
Working With Crystals, Shirley o'Donoghue
Working With Natural Energy, Shirley o'Donoghue
Working With the Merlin, Geoff Hughes
Your Talking Pet, Ann Walker
The Zodiac Experience, Patricia Crowther

FREE detailed catalogue and FREE 'Inspiration' magazine
Contact: Capall Bann Publishing, Auton Farm, Milverton, Somerset, TA4 1NE